Something to Say?
Say It Well!

Something to Say?
Say It Well!

A Pastor's Manual for Preaching

H. Mark Abbott

WIPF & STOCK · Eugene, Oregon

Wipf and Stock Publishers
199 W 8th Ave, Suite 3
Eugene, OR 97401

Something to Say? Say It Well!
A Pastor's Manual for Preaching
By Abbott, H. Mark
Copyright©2011 by Abbott, H. Mark
ISBN 13: 978-1-62564-734-4
Publication date 3/6/2014
Previously published by WinePress Publishing, 2011

Contents

Introduction vii

1. Scared of Speaking in Public? 1
2. That's Biblical!. 13
3. The Bible in One Hand and a Newspaper in the Other . . . 25
4. What's the Big Idea? 33
5. How Will I Have Enough to Say? 41
6. Does It Hang Together? 51
7. Start with an Earthquake and Build to a Climax! 63
8. Language Fit to be Spoken 73
9. Glow Over It 81
10. Deliver that Baby! 85

Appendix A: Having Something to Say and Saying
    It Well at Weddings and Memorials 97
Appendix B: Two Sample Sermons 101
    "Hope in Hard Times"
    "Undated Hope"
Works Cited 127

Introduction

I'M A FORTY-TWO-YEAR practitioner of the art of public speaking both as pastor and homiletics teacher. I have preached several hundred sermons and listened critically, that is reflectively, to a few hundred student sermons. I also believe passionately that, despite contemporary questions about its effectiveness, public proclamation of God's truth is a divinely chosen means of communicating God's own self with men and women.

This book is an attempt to distill and share some of what I've learned into a manual for preachers and other public speakers in a Christian context. I believe would-be preachers, pastors, as well as other Christian leaders, will find a practical primer useful for learning the art of and improving public speaking.

A wide variety of good books on various aspects of preaching exists, including several I've used for assigned readings in homiletics classes and several I quote in these chapters. Many are excellent resources. However, they are seldom written by pastoral practitioners, people who have to apply what they teach Sunday after Sunday with the same congregation.

When I recently had a surgical procedure done, I was interested in knowing how often and how successfully the doctor had done the particular operation. I recognize that some long-time pastoral practitioners of the art of public speaking may be stuck in ruts that do not communicate well today. However, I continue to work hard to connect with the people week after week. I find I do some of my best preaching when I am teaching others to preach.

This is not primarily an academic volume, but a readable book accessible to a wide range of Christian communicators. I hope this resource can be used to assist in the teaching of preaching. At the same time I hope it will serve as a refresher for those in ministry and lay leaders called upon to teach and speak in various settings.

In my years of preaching and teaching, I've concluded that all I know and want to share with others on the subject can be condensed into two basic themes: One, Having something to say and, two, saying it well.

These are at the human core of preaching. Yes, God works through preaching. I believe that and I hope you do also. But what must WE do when we preach? I hope we have something to say that is from God and based in the Bible. Communicating that God-given, Bible-based word effectively is the preacher's challenge.

I have broken down these two basic elements into ten chapters. At the end of each chapter is a short, practical "Reflection" section.

One of my homiletics teaching practices is to work not just with preaching theory. Often I also move inductively from sermon manuscript back to preaching principles. Thus, I have included an appendix with two of my sermon manuscripts, illustrating among other things, at least two different ways to structure sermons. Since one public speaking challenge for Christian leaders is special events, I also included an appendix titled, "Having Something to Say and Saying It Well: Weddings and Memorial Services." In this section I make the case that what we say on such occasions should be primarily based on our theology regarding these special events.

While I share what works for me, I am committed to the reality that each preacher must find his or her own style. Celebrate it, use it, hone it! Don't just copy someone else's preaching style and methods. As a young preacher/pastor, I began to notice some of my colleagues in ministry acting differently when they preached. They

Introduction

began to use a huge open Bible that was laid across one outstretched hand. Then they paced back and forth on the platform with this open Bible stretched out in front of them. I thought to myself, *Oh dear, that preacher has been to "the seminar!"* A gifted communicator was holding seminars on how to do it—how to do it like he did it. But methods that fit this remarkably skilled preacher made my ordinary "two-talent" colleagues look foolish.

Please use whatever good you can find from these chapters. But be yourself, a disciplined, trained, increasingly skilled self, called, gifted, and used by God to proclaim the Word.

Chapter 1
Scared of Speaking in Public?
Public Speaking is a Challenge!

BONO, LEAD SINGER of U2, was getting ready to speak at a Presidential Prayer Breakfast. "I'm scared stiff," he observed. Then he added, "I usually perform before crowds of at least 20,000." A crowd of a few hundred frightened this skilled public performer, who thinks nothing of appearing before thousands. With most of us who are called to speak in public, it doesn't work that way. A crowd of thousands overwhelms us. Maybe a crowd of a hundred frightens us too.

As a pastor I loved the challenge of preaching Sunday after Sunday to people I knew personally and with whom I shared life at many levels. Thus, I tend to be anxious when speaking before people I don't know or people from a different culture than my own. Since I grew up in India where my parents were missionaries and because I've been on several return visits, I've had the privilege and challenge of speaking cross-culturally. But I'm painfully aware of the hazards that kind of public speaking entails, especially when it takes place through a translator. Having something to say from God and saying it well is a very culture-specific task.

Preaching a few years ago to a group of pastors not in India, but in Burundi, I was trying to describe how God had once helped me preach even when I did not feel well. "My face was pale," I declared. The African translator stopped dead in his tracks and looked at me. Sensing something was wrong, I tried again. "My face became white!" He still looked at me, wondering, I'm sure, why I would make such a big deal of the obvious. Finally, an African church leader well-versed in English idiom told the interpreter, "Tell them, 'He looked sick!'" "Ah!" exclaimed the translator and we were back on track!

With these same pastors, I was talking about how important the creation story of Genesis 1 and 2 is for our lives and ministries. After a few puzzled looks, the same church leader interrupted and told me that the interpreter was using the word for "fable" whenever I used "story." "Is that what you want to say?" he wanted to know. Obviously it was not! We agreed that a better term was the word for "record" to translate "story."

Most pastors and church people don't have to speak in front of 20,000. And many of us will not have to speak in Africa, Asia, or Latin America. But if you're a pastor/preacher, you have to have something to say in front of a few dozen or a few hundred people. And many pastor/preachers have this responsibility Sunday after Sunday. If you're a church staff member, maybe the task is not preaching regularly, but giving a talk or a teaching to a youth group or adult class. Perhaps you're asked to train small-group leaders, or, yes, once in a while, to preach in a worship service.

If you're a lay leader in the church, you may teach a class, share a devotional or testimony, or maybe even fill in for the pastor. Perhaps you'll be asked to give a talk at Rotary or Kiwanis. You may have "the gift of gab" and have no trouble speaking in front of people, or perhaps you find it easy to speak spontaneously in public—but run the risk of saying something you later regret. You may be an introvert (like me) and struggle with public speaking. Maybe you have no problem interacting with a small group of peers, but in front of an audience … Oh dear!

I've been a preaching pastor for the past forty-two years. In three different churches, in suburban, rural-college, and urban congregations, I've preached on average forty-five Sundays most years, spoken outside our church several times a year, given hundreds of wedding and memorial service meditations, taught Bible studies on Sunday or Wednesday evening, and preached and taught in other cultures.

Having something to say which I believed was from God and saying it well has been one of my greatest challenges but has also offered a huge sense of fulfillment. For the past twenty-five years, I taught homiletics and led preaching practicum classes with seminary students. I've listened to budding preachers work through their public speaking anxieties as well as come alongside them in their struggle to have something to say and say it well. I do not personally have "the gift of gab." I do not speak well extemporaneously. Having something to say and saying it well for me is *work*. Public speaking *is* a challenge!

While in seminary many years ago, I was a member of a team that held services in small area churches. I mostly played the piano while someone else did the preaching. I remember the young preacher disclaiming any need for preparation. "Why," he said, "I don't decide what to preach until just a few moments before I stand up. I just open my mouth and let the Lord fill it." I observed, as did many who listened, that what the Lord did was fill his mouth with hot air! The challenge of public speaking whether as a preaching pastor or as a lay leader invites serious preparation so that we, in fact, have something to say and that we say it well.

But Has Public Religious Discourse Passed Its Heyday?

Some say it has. People insist on being entertained. People want to see something on a screen. Many public presentations involve power point, videos, even big-screen magnification of the speaker. If you have something to say, we're told, make a video, give people something to see and engage with.

One of the essentials for effective communication today, says popular author and professor of preaching, Leonard Sweet, is that it be "Image-Rich." EPIC is Sweet's acronym. E-Experiential; P-Participatory, I-Image-rich; E-Experiential (Sweet, 2007).

There are also voices within the church seriously questioning the role of preaching as we have known it. Doug Pagitt, a pastor and author, disparagingly refers to "speaching," and calls for a more participatory, sharing experience in which the congregation pools its insights along the lines of an idea thrown out by the leader (Pagitt, 2005).

Maybe Leonard Sweet and Doug Pagitt are right in their critique of a traditional approach to preaching. Maybe public religious speaking in the traditional manner has passed its heyday.

But even if we do use visual images and other high-tech media, we still must have something worthwhile to communicate. Even when preachers do foster a more participatory environment, we still need to have something to say. "Bells and whistles" and audience involvement don't compensate, at least over time, for not having something to say. Pastors and other public speakers in the church are, after all, people who are called to communicate in clear, contemporary, and convincing ways what God has said. (By the way, I do believe in using appropriate technological resources that enhance what I have to say. But they're not a substitute for having something to say.)

Saying well what we have to say should involve an appropriate desired outcome of public speaking and teaching. Do we just want to make an impression regarding how eloquent and creative we are, or how effective we are with high-tech presentations, or do we want people to hear, experience, and respond to God?

Preaching and Leading

Sometimes today preaching/teaching is subordinated and minimized under the role of pastoral leadership. Multiplied books in recent years are aimed at making the pastor a stronger, more effective leader, many of them minimizing the centrality of public communication in church leadership. Michael Quicke, homiletics professor and author complains, "I am deeply concerned about the lack of explicit attention given to preaching's role in Christian leadership. Most writing on Christian leadership omits preaching, and most books on preaching leave out leadership." Quicke continues, "Preaching has become a small cog in the ecclesiastical machinery, turning in response to the driving momentum of larger leadership forces." The result this author observes has been "thin-blooded preaching," which, he says, "misses out on leadership" (Quicke, 2006, p.33)

By contrast, Quicke appeals for "full-blooded preaching today. Instead of the preacher's role being emasculated as chaplain to individual needs and cheerleader to organizational machismo, it must regain its God-given purpose, preaching ... to confront church and culture with the gospel" (Quicke, 2006, p. 43). He continues, "You can lead without preaching (Romans 12:8) but you cannot preach biblically without leading." (Quicke, 2006, p.60)

Preaching and Human Instrumentality

After more than four decades of pastoral preaching, I affirm that leading people through full-blooded preaching requires pastors and other Christian communicators to return again and again to the divine choice of incarnation as God's primary mode of communication. Incarnation and human instrumentality are one of two core themes in understanding and practicing full-blooded preaching.

The story of what God has done for men and women is the story of God working through human beings. God became incarnate or en-fleshed in the works and words of mere mortals. That's what God did with the prophets of ancient Israel, the writers of our Bible books, and the apostles of the early church. Incarnation is supremely evident in Jesus Himself. Incarnation is the most basic way God communicates.

The classic understanding of preaching is communication of truth through personality. Preaching and other kinds of Christian communication are embodied messages. Having something to say from God and saying it well is God working through the preacher. Preaching is the principle of incarnation in action.

That is why preparing to preach involves preparing the preacher. Embodied messages spring from who the preacher is and how the Spirit is forming the preacher's own life. Having something to say consists not only of careful exegesis and practiced delivery, but also being a person in whom God is vitally at work.

God Has Chosen to Use "the Foolishness of Preaching" to Communicate Christ

Another theme of "full-blooded preaching" is God's choice of this means of communicating the Gospel. The apostle Paul wrote to believers in Corinth, "God decided through the foolishness of our proclamation to save those who believe" (1 Corinthians 1:21). If God is using preaching to accomplish His purposes, then more is happening in this communication than what meets the eye. God's Spirit is at work blessing what we have to say (if it is in accord with what God has said) and blessing our often inadequate efforts to say it well.

Darrell Johnson, who taught preaching at Regent College in Vancouver, BC, blessed pastors departing from a pastors' conference with what he called "The Pastors' Syllogism."

1. When *the* Preacher speaks, something happens.
2. When preachers speak *the* Preacher's Speech, *the* Preacher speaks.
3. When preachers speak, something happens.

The Preacher Mr. Johnson was talking about is God and the Word from God. When preachers let *the* Preacher's Word be heard, *the* Preacher speaks. And when *the* Preacher speaks through the human preacher, something happens!

Arthur John Gossip, outstanding Scots preacher of another generation, had a full week of pastoral responsibilities. He had not been able to give his usual time to preparing the Sunday sermon. Gossip tells of preparing to mount the pulpit on Sunday morning. (You know the fortress-like pulpits in many British sanctuaries.) The preacher sensed Christ at the bend in the pulpit stairs. "Gossip, is that the best you can do for me this week?" asked Jesus. "Yes, Lord, this week it is the best I can do," Gossip responded. The preacher reported that in His Hands that Sunday, this inadequate sermon became a trumpet.

So it is my deep conviction that preachers and other public speakers need to have something to say, but that we must be convinced this "something to say" comes from God.

Four Convictions for Christian Communicators

Having something to say from God for Christian communicators involves at least the following convictions (which I'll develop further in subsequent chapters).

First, have something to say which arises out of the text of Scripture. Of course, that text or passage of Scripture is carefully and wisely interpreted. If the preacher speaks more topically rather than expounding on a text, he or she will make it clear that the message is in harmony with the Bible, again carefully and wisely interpreted. How else can we hope to have a word from God?

But quoting reams of Bible by itself does not make a sermon or a lesson biblical or Christian. These questions need to be asked consistently.

- ➢ Does what we have to say express what the Bible passage, understood in its context, as well as the wider scope of Scripture teaches?
- ➢ Are we opening up the text of Scripture?
- ➢ Are we allowing the text to lead the message?
- ➢ Are we simply imposing our ideas and/or the topic for the day on the passage?

Second, connect with the needs and life experiences of your listeners. A preacher, someone has observed, should hold the Bible in one hand and the newspaper in the other. The prophets of ancient Israel did not speak their message into a vacuum, but into specific situations in the lives of the people of their age. Paul and other apostles wrote letters to the early churches and their leaders to respond to specific situations in that time and in those places. Michael Quicke challenges us to ask, "Could this sermon have been preached fifty years ago?" If so, it is too generic and nonspecific (Quicke, 2006, p.37).

Third, we need to have something to say that has one clear message. We should be able to summarize this one clear message in a single active sentence. Some call this "the big idea." If we don't have a clear understanding of our big idea, what we say will be heard as scattered, unfocused, and ineffective. "How many points should a sermon have?" someone asked a famous preacher. "At least one," was the reply.

Are we convinced that the big idea of a message is important? Are we passionate about it? Why should anyone else be vitally interested if we are not?

My experience in preaching and in teaching would-be preachers is that the big idea is at the heart of effective preaching.

Fourth, include materials supporting and expanding the big idea in concrete ways which connect with listeners. Some questions to ask:

> Where can we find materials to support the big idea?
> How will we have enough to say?
> Is it OK to tell stories from our own lives?
> Is it OK to borrow other people's ideas?
> How much should I quote other people?
> And if I do quote how should I do it?

Having something to say which I'm convinced is from God is not the end product in public speaking. I've heard preachers who had done their homework well. These preachers did have some good things to say. But I wished they had let me arrange their content in a sequence which would communicate more effectively with their listeners.

Five Factors for Good Communication

Saying well what we have to say, also essential for good communication, involves at least the following five factors.

Scared of Speaking in Public?

First, order thought-blocks to communicate effectively. Structuring what we have to say may be almost as important as having something to say. Valuable content is often wasted by a scattered and disconnected shape to the message. A coherent structure arises out of a clear understanding of the big idea. Not being able to state what we have to say in a single sentence tends to produce an "all-over-the-map" structure, leaving people wondering, *Now what was the point of all that?*

Second, a strong start and a strong finish. We have only a few opening moments, probably at the most two minutes, to draw people in and convince them that what we have to say is worth paying attention to. If it used to be true that people came to church and sat on the edge of their seats waiting for what the pastor would say, it is no longer the case. Right up front we need to engage, connect, and promise something worthwhile.

Furthermore, we have a problem if the last thing remembered is the talk fizzled or continued beyond most people's attention span. Public speakers should start with an earthquake and build to a climax.

Third, choose concrete and clear language. Some speakers seem to think authenticity requires us to communicate with the first words that come to mind. But words are the tools of a communicator. Why use an axe when a chisel will do better? Why use a saw that makes a mess rather than accomplishing its purpose? On the other hand, if we sound like we're merely reading words off a page, words written to be read and not primarily heard, we miss the boat with effective oral communication. Most contemporary people cope with being read to for only a relatively short period of time. If we major in clear, oral communication, we'll find that short words and short sentences are vital for saying well what we have to say.

Fourth, go over what we have prepared until it becomes a part of us. William Sangster, British preacher of another generation, used to counsel preachers to "glow over it" (Sangster, 1958). What we've prepared must catch fire with us or it will not burn in the ears of listeners. Then, if we do use a manuscript or notes, we'll not just be reading words off a page. Rather, it will be communication from the speaker's heart and mind to the listeners.

Finally, engage our body's resources to be effective vehicles for communication. Authorities tell us that a majority of communication is carried out by non-verbal means. Thus, we must harness our eyes, mouth, hands, posture, yes, our whole bodies, to deliver what we have to say in a way that enhances rather than hinders the message. We want the pace of delivery to engage interest and discourage fast-thinkers from woolgathering. At the same time, we do not want our pace to outstrip people's abilities to hear and receive.

Summary

What to say and how to say it effectively? These key points will be amplified in the chapters to follow.

> - Maybe you are a neophyte, a would-be preacher. Maybe you're scared of speaking in public. I hope to point you in the direction of building preaching skills.
> - Maybe you're a preacher or a church staff member who has considerable experience in preaching. I hope this manual offers a refresher course and a means to reassess and improve a key ministry skill.
> - Maybe you're a lay-Christian who teaches and speaks in front of people. I want to share with you some concrete ways of enhancing what you have to say and saying it even better.

Scared of speaking in public? Let's hope we never become lackadaisical about the challenge and responsibility of speaking God's truth in public. But maybe we can move beyond just being scared to a healthy respect for the responsibility of speaking for God to God's people. And maybe we can recapture a greater confidence in what God can and will do through the spoken word.

Reflection

"If preaching were a Dow-Jones company," writes Kenton Anderson, "its stock would be down, but with a strong 'buy' recommendation. Preaching is not going away. The future is still bright. A renewed emphasis on preaching, a different kind of preaching, is beginning to be felt among younger leaders in the church" (Anderson, 2006, p. 29).

1. What do you think about this statement?
2. Does it square with your experience of listening to preaching today?

Chapter 2

That's Biblical!
Most Preachers Believe They Should Preach Biblically, but What Does That Mean?

MANY YEARS AGO, a church overseer had a habit that both fascinated and irked me. When he told us what he thought about an issue and what we should be doing under his supervision, he concluded by thundering, "And that's biblical!" The subtext of this church leader's declaration was "So don't question what I am saying!"

Clothing what we think is true in the garb of biblical authority to give our opinion added weight has a long and often inglorious history. When this leader made that pronouncement, I often thought, *But you're just telling us what you think! In what sense is that biblical?*

On vacation, my wife and I slipped into a large church to worship on Sunday. The founding pastor was back in town and was preaching that Sunday. He read Romans 12:1 and 2, but thereafter never referred to this well-known passage in his otherwise interesting message. It was a topical message with a biblical passage as a pretext or a jumping-off place. That was not preaching biblically!

While not all public speaking in Christian contexts must open up a passage of Scripture, all that we say in public should be in accord with the witness of the Bible. But if we are called to preach or teach in a Christian setting, the majority of our messages should faithfully open up the text of the Bible so that our listeners understand both what was heard and read in ancient times, and how that applies to our lives and situations today.

Old Testament Prophets

The prophets of the Old Testament were messengers who applied God's word to life situations they saw around them. Prophets like Jeremiah were called "to go to all to whom I send you, and… speak whatever I command you" (Jeremiah 1:7). Rough-hewn prophets like farmer-preacher, Amos, saw a day coming when there would be a famine "not of bread, or a thirst for water, but of hearing the words of the Lord." Amos envisions people "running to and fro seeking the word of the Lord" without success (Amos 8:12). Ancient Hebrew prophets help us see our role as contemporary "prophets."

Strong Heritage in Church History

The high point of ancient preaching was the fourth century. John Chrysostrum, Ambrose, and Augustine were eloquent preachers as well as church leaders. In the early medieval period, preaching declined until a scholastic age renaissance led by powerful preachers such as Bernard of Clairvaux, Thomas Aquinas, and Hildegard of Bingen. Preaching orders of monks, the Dominicans and Franciscans, along with the great Celtic preachers kept oral proclamation of the Gospel alive.

The sixteenth-century Protestant Reformation reawakened the church to the centrality of Scripture not only for Christian doctrine, but for Christian preaching and teaching. Martin Luther went so far as to argue that "preaching plays a role that not even Scripture can play, for preaching gives God an audible voice." If that sounds like hyperbole, think of how amazing it is if only partially true! John Calvin went so far as to assert that "God does not wish to be heard but by the voice of His ministers" (Sittser, 2010, p. 222).

The prime preacher of the eighteenth century Wesleyan Revival declared himself to be "a man of one book." Of course, that wasn't quite true! John Wesley read widely from the writings of the early church fathers to the philosophers of his day. Wesley was actually a man of many books. But the Bible played an absolutely central role in his life and ministry. While not an expositional preacher as I would define it, Wesley referenced Scripture heavily in his voluminous preaching and writing.

Contemporary Voices Appeal for Strong Biblical Preaching

Baptist pastor and professor, Michael Quicke, calling for strong preaching-leading, makes this vigorous appeal.

> Rather than sleepwalking through a text, plodding through exegesis, interpretation, and design, preachers should immerse themselves in Scripture's dynamic that continuously leads people forward. Preaching Scripture is like plunging into a fast-flowing river. Instead of generic catchall sermons that can anesthetize Scripture's challenge and smother its creativity, preachers must engage in lively exegesis and interpretation for their own situations. No more dulled two-edged swords.
> —Quicke, 2006, p. 55

N.T. Wright, Anglican scholar and church leader, challenges us to a high view of the preached word.

> Just as some of the Reformers spoke of the sacraments as God's "visible words," so sermons are supposed to be "audible sacraments."...They are not simply for the conveying of information... They are not simply for exhortation, still less for entertainment. They are supposed to be one of the moments in regular Christian living when heaven and earth meet...God's word is once again audible to the heart as well as the other ears.
> —Wright, 2005, p. 139

The prophets of ancient Israel, preachers of the early church, and high periods in Christian history, along with contemporary voices, call us to preaching based in the text of Scripture. How then, are we to engage in biblical preaching and teaching which effectively opens up the strong and transformational Word of God?

Biblical preaching does not require "oral exegesis," a verse by verse commentary, which is what some think expository preaching is all about. These attempts to be biblical can become dull, tedious, and a turn-off in our entertainment-oriented, screen-fixated age.

Biblical preaching is also not based on the volume of Bible verses quoted. Have you observed that you can find Bible verses to quote on both sides of many issues? Have you heard preachers quote multiple verses, but out of context, thus misusing the Bible? Biblical preaching is driven by what the text said to its ancient hearers interpreted carefully and wisely in its ancient context and applied across centuries and cultures to contemporary hearers.

The Bible is more like a novel than an encyclopedia. In *Encyclopedia Britannica* or even on Wikipedia, you can dip into a single page for a particular piece of information. The encyclopedia serves its purpose. But in a novel, every part of the plot relates to every other part of the plot. The storyline runs throughout the book. This is the case with the Bible. It is not a collection of mottos into which we dip to prove our point, but rather a story with an overall plot and sub-stories with their own messages. Poetic and wisdom literature as well as letters and law are part of the story. And the whole story is interrelated.

Selecting a Bible Passage on Which to Preach

When we talk about biblical preaching, we assume some criteria for selecting the passage for a particular message. How do we decide?

Most mainline church pastors today work with the lectionary, or standard set of assigned readings from Psalms, Old Testament, Gospels, and Epistles for that Sunday. I personally find lectionary preaching useful and helpful to listeners, some of whom will follow and read ahead with you.

Lectionary preaching fosters a treatment of the whole story of salvation over the course of a year. At the same time, lectionary preaching can feel restrictive. The lectionary is not divinely inspired and sometimes omits significant sections of the Bible. Furthermore, attempts to link passages assigned for the Sunday can result in an artificial twisting of texts to make connections. I frequently used the lectionary as a guide during summer months and as a resource for preaching that follows the church calendar. (For a complete listing of Revised Common Lectionary readings go to http://lectionary.library.Vanderbilt.edu/)

That leads me to observe that biblical preaching can and should offer an annual retelling of the great story of Jesus. This is what we do when text selection is guided by the church year. We shortchange our people if we do not take them from Advent through Christmas and Epiphany, then through Lent and Easter, and finally to Ascension and Pentecost. We shortchange our people if we arrive at Easter Sunday without walking solemnly through Lent and Holy Week.

Some evangelical pastors work with books of the Bible, preaching through extended passages of Scripture. While this can be powerful preaching, beware getting bogged down in minutia and missing the big picture. In my first year or two of preaching, I decided that people needed to know Romans. And so, Romans we did, Sunday after Sunday. After about three months of plowing as deep as I knew how, one of our members said to me, "Pastor, how long do we have to do this?" It was clear my flock needed a break from Romans.

A variation on entire book studies is a series on an extended section of Scripture, such as the Ten Commandments or the Sermon on the Mount.

Frequently today, preachers begin with a topical framework then move to find Scripture passages to support the topic's elements. The key issue here is whether I force the theme onto the chosen passage or indeed let the passage speak in its ancient context and then to the contemporary context. Biblical preaching requires me to let the passage direct the focus and emphasis of the sermon rather than letting the topic occupy center stage, somewhat supported by the background passage.

Since I have recently retired after forty-two years in pastoral ministry, I have the opportunity of visiting other churches and listening to a range of preaching on Sundays. I observe a tendency among some of my colleagues to try to shoehorn an assigned or predetermined topic into a passage of Scripture. Recently I heard a preacher say some interesting things which he tried to base in a familiar passage. However, the sermon missed the key themes of that passage, settling for a phrase or two which he used to back up his thematic message.

Sometimes I hear a brief and shallow reference to the text, often without opening up its context. The sermon, then, is mostly the preacher's own agenda. The commendable desire here is to be relevant and scratch folks where they itch. After all, in today's consumer oriented church culture, isn't that what will bring people back? So I've heard "Six (or was it 8) ways to have a happy marriage" with a bit of Bible tacked on at the end.

Let the text speak!

Two Approaches to Biblical Preaching

The preacher has settled on the passage of Scripture. But now, how to handle it so that God speaks clearly and powerfully through His Word? Truly biblical preaching involves one or both of the following approaches.

First, open up a particular Bible passage. Its immediate and wider context is shown so that what the ancient writer intended is understood and then applied to the contemporary context. This allows God to speak through a faithful exposition of a Scripture.

Two hazards in this approach can be, biblical myopia, short-sightedness regarding the bigger picture of the Bible; and a lack of connection with contemporary life as experienced by listeners.

In homiletics class one year I highlighted the Hittites as biblical people today's church attendees really aren't interested in knowing about. "Who cares about the Hittites today?" I asked. A student took up the challenge and preached a whole sermon on the Hittites. Actually he proved my point. The sermon was very biblical and had some flashes of interest, but did not connect with contemporary life.

Second, open up a biblical theme. Pull together a series of passages through which a theme is developed. This is a method popularized by mega-church pastor-preacher, Rick Warren, and one widely used in evangelical churches. A potential hazard of this use of Scripture, however, is that it may not adequately consider the context out of which a verse, or verses, is quoted, thus missing their special contribution to the overall plotline of the biblical story. Any text ripped from its context can become a pretext for saying merely what the preacher wants to say.

Beware of consistently leapfrogging through the Bible without a close reading of any particular passage! How preachers use the Bible models either a wholesome or hazardous use of Holy Scripture for their congregations. Our listeners take their cue on how to use the Bible from us.

A Note about Hermeneutics

While hermeneutics, or biblical interpretation, is beyond the scope of this volume, when working to interpret and apply a particular passage of Scripture, we do well to ask at least three questions. What does it say? What does it mean? What does it mean to me and to us?

What Does It Say?

In other words, what did the passage of Scripture in question say to the people who first heard or read it? This is the essential step of observation. Rather than imposing twenty-first century ideas upon the Bible, we need to allow Scripture to speak on its own terms. Some understanding of the passage's historical context is important for understanding what it was saying to its original hearers or readers. Biblical aids, such as commentaries and Bible dictionaries will help us here. But start by close and careful listening to what the text of Scripture says without immediately bringing twenty-first century baggage to it.

Investing ourselves in observation is what Michael Quicke calls "immersion into Scripture," which he says "is the way to begin doing exegesis" (Quicke, 2006, p. 166). In exegesis preachers pay close attention to what God's Word means in its original context in order to ground their sermons on God's authoritative word.

The temptation of most preachers is to short-circuit the observation process, thus moving too quickly to interpretation and application. We may think we know what the passage means. But do we really? Some of us also leap directly and prematurely into the final step, application.

Probing below the first level of what we think a passage is saying to something deeper enriches a sermon. Instead of just preaching the David and Goliath story (1 Samuel 17) the way I usually presented it (who are the "giants" in our lives?), I was recently able to connect with deeper, truer-to-the-text levels of observation. I observed that Goliath is only once called a "giant" but more often "Philistine" and one who defies the armies of God. Maybe the original author is not stressing the "giant" aspect as much as the Philistine-enemy-of-God role of Goliath.

Furthermore, I have often not carefully observed David's dismissing of traditional weapons for fighting the Philistine champion. Maybe there's a model for twenty-first-century confrontation of champions of evil. We don't use the enemy's weapons when we fight enemies of God.

What did the passage of Scripture in question say to the people who first heard or read it? Observe, observe, observe!

What Does It Mean?

This step of interpretation should follow after seriously working with the observation step. When we ask what a Bible passage means, we ask sub-questions.

First ask, *What genre or kind of literature is this?* For example, if the passage is poetry, it is full of images and clearly should be interpreted symbolically. This is also true with many of the apocalyptic and prophetic passages. When we work with this genre, are we helping people see, hear, and feel, rather than just analyze and understand?

If the passage is from wisdom literature, we remind ourselves that this genre involves statements of probability or likelihood, not promises. Most often, a proverb, for example, will say that if we do something, there is a strong likelihood that a certain result will follow. If we "train up a child in the way he should go," there is a strong likelihood, but no guarantee, that "when he is old he will not depart from that training" (Proverbs 22:6).

If the passage is story or narrative, we listen to the plot, allowing Bible characters to serve as mirrors for us, not necessarily models of good and right behavior.

In preaching from a biblical narrative, we also should beware of the pitfall of moralism, which leaps from "Abraham did this or that" to "therefore we must ..." A preacher used the story of Jesus reconnecting with Peter in John 21. The preacher had the usual three points, using three elements of the conversation. But the approach was one of moralizing.

"Do you love me?" Do we love Him?

"Yes Lord!" This should be our response.

"Feed my sheep." We have a task.

Instead of resorting merely to moralizing and exhorting, try inviting hearers to enter into the plotline and into the characters of these Bible stories. Do we sometimes see ourselves in Peter? What does that look like, feel like? More life transformation comes through encouraging identification with a story and its characters than through offering three principles from it.

If the passage is from an epistle, we remember the New Testament epistles are "occasional literature." That is, they are occasioned by a situation in the author's or recipient person's or church's life. When we read a letter, we listen for the story behind the letter. For example, why did the apostle Paul write to the Philippian Church? Was it because of the dissension he had heard was taking place between Euodia and Syntyche? (Philippians 4:2).

Consider the literary genre of the passage before leaping to an interpretation.

The second question to ask is, *How does the particular passage fit into the wider context?* For example, what larger story is this specific passage a part of? What went before and what follows? What is Jesus saying and doing immediately before and after a particular incident or teaching? For example, listening carefully to the prelude to Luke's wonderful set of parables about lost things and a lost son sheds light on why Jesus told these stories (Luke 15:1-3). The parables about lost things and two lost sons are about good people who do not want to "welcome sinners and eat with them." These parables are not just about what was lost and found, but about people who really do not care whether or not the lost are found.

Here's another example of carefully considering the context of a text. Linking Jesus' exhortation to the disciple to "deny himself, and take up his cross and follow me," with the previous paragraphs in Mark's gospel connects the master's identity of suffering servant (Mark 8:30-33) with the identity of the disciple. The identity of a disciple of Jesus is one who follows the Master's model, following Him even to death (Mark 8:34-38).

Beware of merely dipping into the text of Scripture for an isolated verse or paragraph without considering the context. We often call this "proof texting," using a text to prove a point or make a case—but using it out of context.

One preacher's sermon, titled "Four Anchors" was based on Acts 27:29. The passage describes Paul's ordeal on board ship and letting out anchors in the storm. The four anchors identified by the preacher were family, friends, work, and church. The sermon may have been practical, but the text did not support the message any more than if it had come from Moby Dick. Not only was the preacher proof texting, but was guilty of eisogesis, that is *reading into* the text what the preacher wanted to say rather than exegesis, or *drawing out* what the text is actually saying.

Third, ask, *What do the specific words before us mean?* Word studies are aided by multiplied Bible-study tools available today. A good commentary or Bible dictionary will help us go behind words on a page to the meaning of those words in ancient times.

But in word studies, a general rule is to leave the preacher's linguistic analysis in the background. Let your word studies impact your interpretation without taking time for discussing the nuts and bolts of grammar. Parsing Greek verbs in sermons may impress people with the preacher's scholarship. But is that the goal of our preaching? I heard of a pastor search committee which had two requirements for a new leader: Didn't know Greek and hadn't been to the Holy Land. There was some history there!

What Does This Mean to Me or to Us?

Only after the steps of observation and interpretation should we move to application. Leaping to application shortcircuits the process of allowing the passage to speak for itself on its own terms.

The process of application usually asks, What is the biblical principle which may be applied across the centuries to our life today? The Old Testament law put the eating of pork off limits. Does that mean we are required to be vegetarian or at least avoid pork chops, ham, or bacon? Instead, when we get beneath the prohibition of eating pigs to asking why they were forbidden, we understand that this was most likely a health issue. Growing up in India fifty years ago, we didn't eat pork either. It wasn't safe. So the application to us surely has something to do with how we care for our health in what we eat and do not eat.

Application seldom moves directly from the situation in the ancient text to what faces our hearers many hundreds of years later and across major cultural divides. Application usually asks about the principle evident in what the passage meant to its first hearers. Then, we apply that principle to today's situation.

Devout believers used to apply Pauline exhortations about women covering their heads in worship directly from 2,000 years ago to today (1 Corinthians 11:4-6). The application principle, however, is for men and women to conduct themselves and dress with respect when they worship God together.

While I urge us, in our study and preparation to defer the step of application until we have worked at observation and interpretation, this does not mean that all application waits chronologically until the last part of the sermon. Application can and should be interwoven throughout the delivered message. Application is where we most pointedly connect and reconnect with our listeners. Don't wait till the end to do that!

"That's biblical!" my supervisor used to say. But was it? Or was it just the assumption of authority for what he wanted to say? Today's Christian communicators will want to be genuinely biblical in what we have to say. Thus, we will ask the following questions of ourselves:

> ➤ Are we doing justice to the passage or are we twisting it out of context, making it say something not intended by the author or not readily inferred from the plain word of the text?
> ➤ Have we worked with this passage and its context enough?
> ➤ Have we interpreted it carefully and checked our interpretation sufficiently?
> ➤ Are we applying this interpretation across time and culture to contemporary life?
> ➤ Is this segment of God's Word being allowed to speak clearly both to us and to those to whom we are speaking?

Reflection

A very strong statement on the Bible and preaching comes from pastor and professor, Ian Pitt Watson.

> We must preach biblically or not at all. If what I am saying is not rooted in Scripture, then however interesting or edifying it may be, it is not preaching...The sole source of our knowledge of what God has done comes to us through the text of Scripture under the guidance of the Holy Spirit.
> —Pitt-Watson, 1986, p. 24

1. What do we think about this strong statement?
2. Are we prepared to accept its guidance as we think about our preaching?

Chapter 3
The Bible in One Hand and a Newspaper in the Other

NORMAN VINCENT PEALE, a mid-twentieth century preacher, pastor, and author was known for his emphasis on "the power of positive thinking." In the process of an extended ministry, theological conservatives criticized Peale for not being faithful enough to the Bible. But Peale hired an evangelical to direct the operation of a training center he established. One day the director turned to his boss and asked, "Dr. Peale, I was wondering do you know what it means to be 'born again?'"

Norman Vincent Peale became surprisingly angry and shot back, "Yes, I do!"

And that was the end of the conversation.

A week later, Peale reopened the conversation. He said to his operations director, "Your question upset me because you assumed that I did not know what it meant to be 'born again.'" Peale continued, "I was brought up under the same teaching as you. I understand the need for salvation based on the cross of Christ. But it bothered me that evangelicals seemed to love the Bible and care little about people. So I determined that I wouldn't follow their course. I would love people more than the Bible. In retrospect, I acknowledge that in loving people, I've not always honored God's Word as I should have. However, you, evangelicals, have erred on the other side. You've loved the Bible and disregarded people. Maybe we have something to learn from each other" (Johnston, 2001, p. 21).

"We must hold the Bible in one hand and a newspaper in the other," Karl Barth is reported to have urged. It's not one *or* the other, but *both* the Bible *and* the newspaper. In Norman Vincent Peale's terms it is both the Bible and people.

Eugene Peterson tells of struggling to be a preaching pastor "in a territory bordered on one side by a believing (or semi-believing) congregation, on the other side by an indifferent (and occasionally scornful) world, and on the third side by the biblical text that I had promised to faithfully preach and teach."

Peterson reports that he found the Scripture passages he preached "were being rewritten, unconsciously but constantly, in the minds of my parishioners to give sanction to behaviors and values that, more often than not it seemed to me, were in the service of the American way (in which consumerism was conspicuous) rather than the way of the cross (where sacrificial love was prominent)" (Peterson, 1996, p. 340).

Peterson credits the example of theologian/pastor Karl Barth, who, as Peterson puts it, "disentangled gospel spirituality from cultural religion, commending the former and rejecting the latter. As for the world, Barth was immensely knowledgeable but quietly un-intimidated. He knew politics and labor and prisons; but he believed in prayer and Scripture and the cross of Christ" (Peterson, 1996, p. 341).

Having something to say from God requires faithful study and exposition of God's word through the Bible. But how the preacher processes that word and communicates in sermons depends on a careful exposition both of the culture and the congregation. How the Bible is preached also depends on understanding the process of communication. That is where we begin as we consider forces which dramatically influence how we decide what to say and how to say it.

Communication Is Complicated!

Try to unravel a complex, emotion-laden issue via email and we quickly confront the hazards of communication. My rule of thumb, broken at my own peril, is never to hit the send button when I'm angry and never to communicate on emotionally fraught issues via e-mail.

Most pastors are connected to more congregational "grapevines" than they want to be. The information/gossip that loads these communication vehicles regularly has to be decoded, checked out, and sometimes simply ignored. My rule of thumb is not to act on something I hear unless I have it confirmed by at least one other dependable source.

Communication is complex in the everyday work of a pastor. Communication is also complicated even when it is carefully thought out as in a Sunday sermon. Do we know whether or not people actually heard the words the preacher intended to say? Do we know whether or not people actually received the central message the preacher intended to bring? Or was there blockage in the pathway which skewed the communication?

Sometimes I am amazed, even horrified, at feedback from people indicating what they heard from what I said. On the other hand, at times I am stunned at how God used what I said to accomplish a completely different purpose than what I had intended. Human barriers in preacher and listener sometimes block God's Spirit. And sometimes God's Spirit accomplishes the communication of a clear word to an individual in spite of my blunderings and glitches in the communication process.

The Preacher Needs to Be Aware of Himself or Herself

- Am I clear about what I think the text is saying?
- How is my personal prejudice distorting what I say or do not say?
- Am I angry and letting my feelings color what I say and how I say it?
- Do I have integrity with what I am preaching?
- Am I daring to call God's people to something I know nothing about or am thumbing my nose at?

Preacher and homiletics professor, Calvin Miller writes,

> No reasonable book on the subject of preaching can begin with what is said. The force of preaching must begin with who's saying it. The collapse of many religious cable empires in the '80's points to the fact that what is said makes very little difference when compared to the character of the one who is saying it.
> —Miller, 2006, p. 25

What Is Going on in the Pews?

Calvin Miller urges not only the exegeting of the text but also an exegeting of the audience. Says this former preaching pastor, now professor and guest preacher on many Sunday mornings, "The hardest exegesis I do—the exegesis that precedes even analyzing the text—is the work of analyzing the audience. I know that if my audience exegesis goes awry, my exegesis of the text—however brilliant—will not help much" (Miller, 2006, p. 42).

Part of exegeting what is going on in the pews is assessing and responding to the environment in which preaching is taking place. Are people uncomfortably hot or cold? Is there movement in the congregation that is disrupting people's attention? How will I respond to those factors? Are there outside-the-sanctuary noises which are obviously distracting? If people's attention is clearly disrupted by something in the environment, I might as well pause and acknowledge what is going on, if possible working the distraction into the message.

Invite and Respond to Feedback

The preacher also needs to be a listener. One author puts it this way, "Most preachers become preachers because they're convinced they have something to say. But listening is, hands down, the most underrated element of biblical preaching" (Johnston, 2001, p. 169). This kind of listening takes place before, during, and after the sermon.

The Bible in One Hand and a Newspaper in the Other

Some preachers have designated feedback groups or at least trusted listeners who are asked to share how they heard what was communicated.

Haddon Robinson has observed, "The age of the preacher has gone, the age of the communicator has arrived" (Johnston, 2001, p. 149). If so, preachers who want to have something to say from God need to give serious attention to the process of communication.

Expounding the Culture

Today progressives critique conservatives for being stuck in the world of twenty centuries ago, losing touch with what is today. And that is often the case! I sometimes listen to seminary students unravel the details of Greek or Hebrew verbs and find myself asking "Who is going to care about this?" A leading evangelical preaching pastor today complains that "far too many sermons have lots of information about the Bible but are not really biblical preaching because they do not call and enable people to respond to the Word."

Conservatives today complain that progressives, even fellow evangelicals, lose touch with their biblical moorings in an endless quest for relevance. One conservative Web site complains,

> Sermons are rarely more tiresome than when they strive for relevance. Drawing from the latest headlines transforms the preacher into a one-man MacLaughlin Group, a Crossfire without the cross though perhaps with some of the fire, and leave the congregation thinking, "If I wanted Meet the Press, I could have stayed in bed."
>
> —Liethart, 1996

However, another conservative author urges this,

> Biblical communication to a postmodern culture should be approached in the same way that a missionary goes into a foreign culture. No missionary worth his or her salt would enter a field without first doing an exhaustive study of the culture he or she

seeks to reach. The time has come for today's preachers to don the missionary garb.

—Johnston, 2001, p. 10

How do we study the culture? How do we let the newspaper, Internet news, contemporary literature and media, or demographic information impact how we communicate what we have to say from God?

As missionaries to the culture:

- We first look within, seeking to understand ourselves and what we as communicators bring to what we have to say.
- We don't assume the culture is informed or is even interested in what we have to say. Even in evangelical churches, preachers do well to assume biblical illiteracy. People are open and in need, yes! But they're not necessarily interested in what the Bible says. Detailed citations of chapter and verse, dropping biblical-theological terms, assuming people know who wrote what and when, are all recipes for missing the boat in connecting today's listeners to what we have to say.
- We inform ourselves of how our culture thinks. We listen, watch, read popular media. We read fiction. We go to movies. But we do all these things not just as consumers, but as communicators looking for clues to how our culture is processing reality. Find a Web site that offers movie reviews from a faith-based perspective. Try www.cinemainfocus.com. Subscribe to at least one news magazine and one daily newspaper. Use your Google search engine aggressively to check what's out there.
- Do we know how pervasive the impact of postmodernism is on how people think? This is not the place for an exposition of postmodernism. But, like it or not, it is behind the way people think outside of church and inside the church.
- Do we know how pervasive pantheism is in popular spirituality? A recent *New York Times* column, in the context of critiquing the blockbuster movie *Avatar*, offered

trenchant comments on "Hollywood's religion of choice for a generation now" (Douthat, 2009) That "religion of choice" is contemporary pantheism.
- ➢ We're aware of and work at responding to cultural diversity. Especially if our place of ministry is an urban center, we face increasing cultural and ethnic diversity in the community as well as among those who attend services seeking for something that will encourage, comfort, and guide.
- ➢ We're aware of and respond to the events which churn through the popular mind. What is the impact of current regional, national, and global news that is brought into our living rooms and computer screens daily? On Christmas Eve I referenced the tragic shootings of police officers in our area. One "Christmas and Easter" person stopped me to express appreciation for what was only a brief comment. Her daughter recently married a Seattle police officer.

"People have changed address," comments an Australian pastor. "And unless we work out where they are, we will fail to communicate with them" (Johnston, 2001, p. 16).

Assessing the Congregation

Preaching never takes place in a vacuum. The word from God through the text of Scripture is the same regardless of the character of our listeners. But the way we handle that Word and the way it is shaped into a sermon may be dramatically different depending on the congregation.

Consider the impact of geographical subculture on your congregation. When I moved from western New York to Seattle, Washington, one of the most helpful reads suggested to me was *The Nine Nations of North America*, a description of regional subcultures by Joel Garreau. (Garreau, 1981)

Consider the educational level of the congregation to whom you preach. Educational level has a lot to do with vocabulary. Never underestimate people's intelligence, but never overestimate their vocabulary.

Consider the age demographics in the congregation you serve. The word from the Lord needed by mature saints has overlap with, but may not always be identical to, what middle and younger adults are looking for. Diverse ages in the same congregation can be dealt with in how one handles application. But the preacher needs to know what he or she is doing.

Consider denominational/theological issues. Yes, the era of the denomination has mostly passed, and the era of the local church is here. However, we need to be sensitive to corporate expectations when we preach. For example, in some congregations the issue of inclusive language is not just an issue of political correctness, but a deeper theological concern. Authors whom I cite in a message depend to some extent on the theological and denominational biases of those to whom I am preaching. Quoting Brian McLaren, or another "emergent" guru, or citing Jim Wallis from *Sojourners* may set up insurmountable barriers. C.S. Lewis, on the other hand, remarkably authoritative for contemporary evangelicals, may provide strong support for the application I am making.

Having something to say that is worthwhile and from God thus involves serious attention to ourselves and what we bring to the preaching task, to the processes of communication, to the culture, and to the congregation to whom we preach. We never preach in a vacuum. There is always the context of ourselves, communication realities, culture, and congregation.

Reflection

"We must hold the Bible in one hand and a newspaper in the other."

How did the sermon you last preached, the one you are working on right now, or one you heard last Sunday connect with the world of the community and the world of the congregation?

Chapter 4
What's the Big Idea?

SOME OF US are wired for linear thinking. We process information sequentially. We default to lists of ideas. We like clear outlines. But some of us are wired for more global thinking. We think in pictures, images, collages, stories.

Regardless of how we process ideas and how we structure proclamation of the Gospel, it benefits both the preacher and hearers if there is a clear, central idea in the message. This central theme may be unpacked by an outline or described by a picture or in stories. In either case the big question is whether or not the preacher can state the gist of the sermon in a single active sentence.

No, we don't have to follow the old preacher's method, "I tell 'em what I's going to tell 'em. Then I tell 'em.' And then, I tell 'em what I just told 'em." The central theme of a sermon may not even be stated upfront, but is, nevertheless, the heart and core of what the preacher says. On the other hand, if this sermon theme is, in fact, repeated half a dozen times in the sermon, there's a stronger possibility that people will get it, leaving the worship service with something they can hang onto and return to in the days to come.

Charles Simeon, Anglican preacher of the nineteenth century observed, "Any fool can make simple things complex, but it takes a wise person to make complex things simple."

Central to the preaching task is making the "something to say" clear enough to state in a single sentence. Unless the preacher can crystallize the message into this single sentence, it is not likely that people will hear a coherent message. This single sentence in itself is not of utmost importance. But it is a powerful tool to fostering unity in the message. And unity *is* of utmost importance, as we shall see when we come to a later chapter on structuring or shaping the message.

During the first minutes of homiletics classes, I invite students to share what they remember from the past Sunday's sermon. Listening critically, that is, with an awareness of what the preacher is doing, helps to improve one's own preaching. It fascinates me how often preaching students will draw a blank about the primary message of sermons heard only a few days previously. Sometimes they reference a passage of Scripture on which the message was based, but cannot remember what the theme was. Of course, that may speak to inadequate listening. But it may also reveal a poorly focused central theme.

Haddon Robinson, author and preaching professor for many years, may have been the first to coin the phrase "the big idea." But a wide variety of homiletics professors have stressed the same preaching priority, calling it the proposition of the sermon or its main impact. Writes Robinson, "A sermon has many ideas to it, but all of them should grow out of the major idea of the sermon." (Robinson, 2008)

And why should this be so? For one, we organize the sermon around the big idea. Shaping and structuring a sermon depends on the big idea. Again from Robinson, "Take all the parts of a sermon and put them together into a whole, and that whole is the central idea—the big idea—in the sermon" (Robinson, 2008). A later chapter in this book will detail how to structure a sermon. It is sufficient here to observe that effective structure in a sermon depends on a clearly focused big idea.

The big idea also enables us to leave something lasting in the minds of hearers. Listeners don't need to remember the three points of an outline. But preachers hope listeners will remember the main point of the sermon. How many points does a sermon need? At least one!

What's the Big Idea?

How often have we heard the complaint, "I just didn't get anything out of what he was saying." Or, "When she was finished preaching, I didn't know what she had been talking about."

In an interview with PreachingToday.com, Robinson expanded on his theme of the big idea:

> The idea has to be narrow enough to be sharp. It has to be narrow enough to get under your skin as a preacher. It's a clear answer to the question, What exactly am I talking about? If you have a vague idea, if it's too broad, too general, too abstract, it doesn't do anything for you. But when you get one that's sharp enough to get into your soul, that's important.
> —Robinson, undated

Focusing the sermon on a big idea means our sermons are not just oral exegesis or verbal commentary on the text. Sermons which merely proceed line by line with a devotional thought thrown in here and there may work for a Sunday class or belong in a published commentary. But they are not effective biblical sermons.

More specifically, focusing a sermon on a big idea means that it is not just a sermon, for example, on the Twenty-third Psalm. Rather, a message based in Psalm 23 lifts up a big idea drawn from careful study of the passage. Review this familiar Psalm, observing first what it says about God. Then, ask yourself what these characteristics of God mean in your life.

> The Lord is my shepherd, I shall not want. He makes me lie down in green pastures; he leads me beside still waters; he restores my soul. He leads me in the right paths for his name's sake. Even though I walk through the darkest valley, I fear no evil; for you are with me; your rod and your staff—they comfort me.
>
> You prepare a table before me in the presence of my enemies; you anoint my head with oil; my cup overflows. Surely goodness and mercy shall follow me all the days of my life and I shall dwell in the house of the LORD my whole life long.
> —NRSV

Did you observe two pictures of God, shepherd and host? The first picture amplified in the Psalm speaks of care, provision, leadership, constant presence (even in the "darkest valley"). The second image of host paints a picture of welcome, celebration, and security forever. (When the ancient Middle Eastern host invites you to his table, he guarantees your safety.)

What then, does this say about us and how we live our lives? What does it mean to us three millennia later that God is like a good shepherd and like the One who prepares a table before me? Here's at least one big idea statement which can form the basis for a message rooted in Psalm 23, "Because of who God is, we can trust God in all of life and forever."

Similarly we do not preach on the parable of the good Samaritan (Luke 10:25-37) but rather on something like this big idea, "Being a neighbor means providing tangible love and care to the one in need on our life journey." But how do we zero in on and develop this big idea statement as we work with a passage in preparation to preach?

Start with an Exegetical Idea

Close reading of a Scripture passage leads to understanding what that passage was saying to its original hearers. Observe closely and listen with the ears of an ancient Middle Easterner. Use available tools in library and/or Internet. What did these first hearers of this passage understand in their context? Let the text say what it was intended to communicate to its first hearers. Summarize the fruit of that close study in a sentence or two? That is the exegetical idea.

From this exegetical idea, the preacher develops a homiletical idea. The homiletical idea is how he or she intends to proclaim this message for today's hearers. This homiletical big idea will be based in one of the exegetical themes in the passage and will allow these exegetical themes to expand it. The homiletical big idea may vary from sermon to sermon on the same text, depending on the situation and the hearers. But the big idea consistently emerges from the passage and its careful exegesis by the preacher.

What's the Big Idea?

"Preaching," says Quicke, "involves both sound exegesis leading out from the text, expressed in biblical terms and theological language, and a main impact leading to the hearers, expressed in accessible language and attention-grabbing images" (Quicke, 2006, p. 153).

Work with the text in its context until you have an understanding of what it said to its original hearers. Then, ask yourself how you will allow this ancient but always relevant word to speak clearly and concretely to today's hearers. A big idea starts with an exegetical idea.

A Complete Statement with Subject and Complement

"The love of God" or "The danger of dishonesty," for example, are inadequate big idea statements. A complete sentence includes a subject, which expresses what I am talking about. Again, borrowing from Haddon Robinson,

> You can state the subject in terms of a question. That is, you can't preach a sermon on forgiveness. You can preach a sermon on, Why should we forgive? or a sermon on, How do we go about forgiving other people? or, When should we forgive? Should we do it immediately? Should we do it when the other person apologizes or repents? Who should forgive? One of those questions will dominate, and you have to think that through, What's the biblical writer getting at? What's he talking about?
> —Robinson, 2008

If my big idea sentence is based in a complete subject, that same sentence also includes a complement. The complement declares what I'm saying about what I'm talking about. If the subject is a question, the complement is the answer to the question. Then, both the question and the answer become the big idea sentence.

I am writing this sitting on a lanai overlooking the Pacific Ocean in Maui, Hawaii. In that context, here's an illustration of a subject-complement sentence.

Subject: *Because Maui's scenery and climate do not disappoint,*
Complement: *I like to come here as often as I can.*

Or here is another more "spiritual" sample sentence.
Subject: *Reading the Psalms regularly*
Complement: *shapes my vision of God and how I communicate with God.*

Review the above suggested big idea for a sermon based in Psalm 23.
Subject: *Because of who God is*
Complement: *we can trust God in all of life and forever.*

Revisit the big idea for a sermon based in Jesus' parable of the good Samaritan.
Subject: *Being a neighbor means*
Complement: *providing tangible love and care to the one in need in our life journey.*

Take a big idea possibility for a sermon based in the often-quoted John 3:16.
Subject: *The outcome of God's love*
Complement: *is to make life available to the one who believes in Jesus.*

Or think of Lamentations 3:22-23.
Subject: *Because the compassionate faithfulness of God never fails*
Complement: *we can hope in the midst of adversity.*

Thus, an effective biblical sermon is not a line-by-line commentary on the passage. Nor is it a sermon on a one-word idea, like love, mercy, or grace. An effective biblical sermon is based in a complete sentence big idea which grows out of careful exegesis of the passage.

Moving Target

A big idea may be a moving target during earlier stages of message preparation. Sometimes the big idea is clear early on as I think about a message and work with the biblical material. Sometimes

I formulate a big idea, but adjust and fine tune it as the message unfolds under the Holy Spirit's guidance. Sometimes the hardest thing in the preparation of a sermon is to get this big idea in clear focus. However, I suggest that a sermon is not ready to be preached until I can reduce it to this single subject-complement sentence.

Twenty-five plus years of teaching homiletics and listening to in-class preachers has highlighted the absolute centrality of this preaching task. This is important even in a postmodern world which is more interested in a collage of images than in an outline. This is important even though the ultimate goal of preaching is to allow God, not just the preacher, to speak to listeners.

God may, and often does, speak in ways I do not intend. His message will not necessarily fit my big idea statement. However, God wants me to offer my best in preaching preparation, fully aware that God will use it in individuals' lives according to what the Spirit knows they need to hear.

"What's the big idea?" That's a crucial question for a preacher to ask. At least humanly speaking, its answer may depend upon a sermon's effectiveness in connecting and communicating. Thus, it is worth investing blood, sweat, even tears in this preaching task.

"Is your sermon ready?" someone may ask a preacher. A part of the answer to that question is whether or not the prior question, "What's the big idea?" has been satisfactorily answered.

Reflection

Work with the following Scripture passages, developing big idea statements that include both subject and complement:

Psalm 13
Isaiah 49:14-16
Matthew 11:25-30
1 John 1:8-10

Chapter 5

How Will I Have Enough to Say?

IT MAY HAVE been Winston Churchill's shortest speech on record. Churchill, now a national hero, returning to his English prep school, stood at the lectern and in his well-known, gravelly voice spoke slowly. "Never give up! Never give up! Never, ever give up!"

Churchill returned to his seat as students erupted in applause. Try that next time you are asked to preach, and you will probably not be invited back!

My father, a missionary for many years in India, was to give a series of messages at a large Christian convention in Kerala, in the deep south of the country. When he first preached, after finishing his usual half-hour sermon, an event leader told him, "If you cannot preach longer than that, we will have to put up someone else to preach when you are finished." The next time it was my father's turn to preach, he used the rest of the series he had prepared. That satisfied expectations. After all, when you have walked for hours to listen to God's Word preached, you don't expect it to be over in half an hour.

Decades later, visiting in India, I was invited to bring "words of greeting" to a Christian gathering in Hyderabad. What I did not know is that this meant a mini-sermon. I spoke for about five minutes and brought what I thought were "words of greeting." When I sat down the Indian leader of the assembly kindly observed that this preacher finished preaching before he began. The next time I spoke in that setting I made sure I had more to say.

Often inexperienced students in homiletics classes wonder if they'll have enough to say. Other students, whose preaching models are forty-five minutes to an hour sermons wonder how they can condense what they have to say to the fifteen to twenty minute limit of a preaching lab setting. It's important to remember the following:

1. Having something to say is not just restating the big idea in a dozen different ways.
2. Having something to say is not just lining up several Bible passages that seem to say the same thing.
3. Having something to say is not just beating people over the head with exhortations.

By the way, how do you respond when told over and over what to do? If you are anything like me, you withdraw, avoid, even resist. Let's find other ways to share what God has laid on our hearts than to merely exhort, exhort, exhort. Incorporating materials which support and expand the big idea in concrete ways will help listeners connect with the message in a deeper way.

Biblical Materials

The following are kinds of materials, which not only make the sermon of presentable length, but drive home and illustrate the big idea.

One type of biblical material is *contextual references*. These help set the particular passage in its context. Take for example, a message on the importance of reconciliation between separated believers based in Philippians 4:2-3. The preacher may highlight the emphasis in Philippians as a whole on the importance of unity among believers (see Philippians 2:1-5).

A message based on the prodigal son parable should reference Luke 15:1-2, which specifies Jesus' audience and thus His focus in this parable. This contextual material helps to turn the spotlight not just on the son who had gone astray, but on the son who had never left the Father's house, but did not share the Father's heart.

The preacher may also cite *key parallel passages*, which may amplify and/or illustrate the big idea of the message. For example, it would not be unusual for a preacher basing a sermon on Psalm 23 to cite Jesus' John 10 statement, "I am the Good Shepherd. The Good Shepherd lays down his life for the sheep" (John 10:11).

In a recent message titled, "How Does the Story End?" based in Revelation 21 and 22, I compared the healing leaves from the tree of life in the urban garden toward which our great story moves (Revelation 22:1-2) with leaves in the garden of Eden, where the great story begins (Genesis 2).

The preacher may use *Bible stories as illustrations* of the big idea. The Bible is full of powerful stories that deserve to be told and retold. The parables of Jesus may serve the same purpose. Take for example a message based in the Lord's Prayer segment on receiving and passing on forgiveness (Matthew 6:12). The preacher could retell the marvelous parable of the king's servant who was forgiven an un-payable debt, but refused to forgive his fellow servant's indebtedness to him (Matthew 18:23-35).

Particularly when preaching cross-culturally, preachers will mine the stories of the Bible. These illustrations work well in place of the culturally conditioned story illustrations we tend to use with American audiences.

Also in the preacher's resource of materials is *restatement*. Restatement may be as simple as saying "in other words ..." or citing how *The Message* paraphrase by Eugene Peterson renders the passage. It could also take the form of metaphor or simile. For example:

> For a believer to refuse to forgive is like having one's mortgage paid, but refusing to forgive the cost of a bag of groceries.

Often a series of restatements expressed in parallel language will make the point concrete and clear.

Another resource in the effective preacher's arsenal is *explanation/definition/facts*. Especially in a well-educated, science-oriented culture, information is weighty. But when we cite what we regard as facts, let's make sure they are right. Preaching in the east, I was making the case that a small oversight can lead to a major catastrophe. I reported that according to the media responsibility for a recent plane crash was charged to a maintenance flaw. After the service, a person introduced himself to me as the chief of maintenance at that particular airport. He wanted me to know in no uncertain terms that there had been no maintenance flaw in this case! Use the Internet to check facts. It's amazing what a Google search will unearth.

Why and When to Quote?

Along with biblical supplements, some preachers support their case with quotations. But why quote? In contrast to other teachers of His day, wasn't Jesus known as one who did not cite other rabbis to make His case? But you and I are not Jesus!

Why and when to quote? When someone else says it better than you can. These are pithy sayings which may drive home an idea or argument. They may incorporate a memorable image or picture. I love the Elizabeth Barrett Browning lines,

> Earth's cramm'd with heaven,
> And every common bush aglow with God.
> But only he who sees takes off his shoes,
> The rest sit round and pluck blackberries.

But quoting lengthy segments of poetry has diminishing impact unless the preacher is particularly adept at it. Quoting very much of anything is usually not effective unless it is reinforced by PowerPoint or handed-out notes. The ear does not follow lengthy sentences designed to be read, not listened to.

Why and when to quote? When citing an authority strengthens your case. St. Augustine has a powerful sentence, "God loves each of us as if there were only one of us to love."

I like to quote John Wesley, who carries weight with my kind of folks. "I lived a hair-breadth from Calvinism all my life so that I could be a Christian."

Be careful not to claim others' words as your own. Plagiarism is using other people's words while claiming them as your own. Plagiarism is dishonest. Plagiarism ignores the incarnational principle on which preaching is based. God wants to speak through you and me and our words. Plagiarism has become increasingly epidemic with the easy availability of famous preachers' sermons on the Internet or in print. Some famous preachers actually market their sermons around key themes and urge those who buy the package to use them verbatim.

How can we profit from others without stealing their ideas/words? Acknowledge when a statement or a story is not your own. If you cannot pin down the exact source for a quote (try Google!) at least say, "A famous person once said …" Or say, "I once heard a story about …"

Don't go into the whole routine of footnote details. Cite briefly. Cite just enough to make the quotation meaningful. But do cite! Preachers who plagiarize will live to experience the biblical adage, "Your sins will find you out!"

The Power of Story

Another source of powerful material heavily used by today's preachers is story. Today's listeners respond to story-telling. It slips under our defenses, "telling it slant" as Eugene Peterson puts it.

There are, however, some who dismiss the impact of story-telling. They may be reacting to an overdose of illustrations, or fabricated and unreal narratives. A college faculty member back east once urged me, "Forget the stories! Just give us the straight biblical teaching."

But the greatest teacher of all, Jesus, was a consummate story teller. In fact, Jesus seldom preached without the use of parables.

Surely Jesus' example makes a strong case for the contemporary value of story-telling.

Furthermore, the Bible itself is "the greatest story ever told," a series of narratives within a great narrative. As Macbeth, one of Shakespeare's pessimists observes, life is "a tale that is told by an idiot full of sound and fury signifying nothing." Revise Macbeth to say: "Life is a tale told by every one of us signifying everything!"

Good story-telling holds attention and reacquires attention. Brain researcher John Medina claims that humans have a ten-minute attention span. After ten minutes, oral communicators need to re-engage listeners. Medina himself is a rapid-paced speaker, using multiple media, reconnecting with listeners at least every ten minutes.

- ➢ Good stories make an idea concrete, "earthing" the idea in real life.
- ➢ Good stories are like a window opened onto truth being addressed.
- ➢ Good stories are like a pause to digest—especially when a message is loaded with content.
- ➢ Good stories appeal to something other than intellect.

Of course motivation to action has an information base. But humans are not only intellectual beings. Motivation includes emotions. Emotions are touched by stories.

A sermon on a biblical narrative can, in fact, be an extended story. Some of the most effective sermons I have heard have been shaped by the contours of the biblical story on which they were based. Sometimes a contemporary story parallels the ancient story, applying it to life as we know it today.

But Where Do Stories Come From?

Yes, you can buy books of illustrations. And yes, you can subscribe to a database of themed stories. But there is nothing like a story from your own life.

How Will I Have Enough to Say?

The times when I cautiously (I was raised in a British boarding school!) opened up a page from my own life, I realized that everyone in the room was listening. *This preacher is a human being like we are. This preacher knows about the kind of life we live!* Sometimes people remember the story but not the sermon. But if the Spirit works through that story to touch human hearts, that's the point of the whole exercise. Here are some cautions about telling stories about your own life.

- Don't *only* tell stories about yourself. Vary the repertoire.
- Don't only tell stories that show you in a good light. Let people hear about failures as well as glowing successes.
- On the other hand, don't confess your faults to the extent that people hear nothing else. I once heard a preacher tell of becoming so angry at his wife that he put his hand through a door. You could almost hear a corporate gasp from the congregation. I suspect most people thought, *You need to go to an anger management group, buddy!*
- Don't say, "Now, to illustrate," or, "Here's a story that will illustrate what I am talking about." Just tell it and let people judge if it illustrates or not.
- At the end, don't over-do application to the theme of the message. If it's a good story, people will get the point without being beaten over the head with it.
- Don't talk about spouse or children without their permission. My deal with my kids was that I would not only get their permission, but compensate them in some small way for being talked about publicly.
- Don't ever betray a confidence to make a powerful story. If people hear in public what they told you in confidence, they will cease to trust you. With many miles and years between, I sometimes felt I could share personal stories from a previous pastorate. Once, recently, I did so only to find that a family from that former church attended that service!

> On the other hand, people may give you permission to protect their identity but retell their story. In fact, a woman I counseled who shared the devastating impact of having an affair urged me to tell people her story while protecting her identity.

But every-Sunday preachers are not likely to have stories from their own life ready each week. At least I don't! Sometimes I have begged, "God, you know I need a story right here in this sermon. Please!"

Where Else to Find Stories

Preachers should be readers who save preaching materials from their reading. Scour newspapers, news magazines, *Readers Digest*, devotional books, novels, movies.

At the end of a book, I jot down topics and page numbers that wait for time to transfer them into my digital file of preaching materials. An effective preacher in my area has a data base of 400-plus collected stories, which he reviews regularly for anecdotes to fit his sermons.

Many preachers carry around a little notebook in which to scribble ideas from life. Our bread and butter is the life that goes on all around us. In that, we are in good company. The prophets of ancient Israel applied God to their contemporary situation. Jesus pointed to common figures of His day to make a point. Look at the sower, the shepherd, the marriage feast, the guy getting mugged on the Jericho Road.

When all else fails, check out Online or print collections of illustrations. But beware, they may and often do sound canned.

Remember

> Let the heart of a message be its big idea.
> Let the skeleton of a message be its structure. (We will get to that in the next chapter.)
> Then, let the skin and flesh of a message be its materials.

Reflection

Have you begun a system for collecting sermon materials? Let it be simple. It can be as simple as a shoe box or a four by six card file. Try carrying around a small notebook in which you jot down ideas during the day. Of course, you could text them to your data base too!

If you haven't started, start now.

Chapter 6
Does It Hang Together?

"I REALLY THOUGHT that sermon had good content. But I wish the preacher had shaped the message so that it hung together better!" Just recently, I said something like that to my wife after listening to a biblically based and enthusiastically delivered sermon. Have you heard reactions to a sermon something like, "I just couldn't get a handle on what the preacher was saying"? A major challenge for preachers is structuring or shaping the raw materials of a message. And whether or not what the preacher has to say is said well depends heavily on this central task. Sermon structure is crucial for having something to say and saying it well.

You've selected the passage and studied it carefully and prayerfully. You've a preliminary big idea sentence in mind based in your understanding of what the passage is saying and how to communicate it to the audience you have in mind. You've begun to collect materials to support and develop this big idea. Now is the time to ask how best to shape the developing sermon. Some preachers begin work on this shaping task early in the process, finding the shaping of the message integral to the whole preparation process. Other preachers find it best to wait till the collection of materials is well along before considering structure.

Shape is movement through the sermon. It is a plan for deciding the sequence of what is said. Writes homiletics professor, Thomas Long, "Form is as important to the flow and direction of a sermon as are the banks of a river to the movement of its currents ... It provides shape and energy to the sermon and thus becomes itself a vital force in how a sermon makes meaning" (Long, 1989, p.92).

Most listeners will not be conscious of how the preacher is shaping the message. We do not want them to be preoccupied with structure. But listeners are aware of whether or not what the preacher said hung together. Structuring a message is a background task. But like a beautiful picture, backgrounds enhance or diminish the impact of a message.

But before we go further, it may be a good time to ask an important question related to the process of structuring a message.

To Manuscript or Not to Manuscript?

This question is often confused with another: When I deliver the sermon, will I do so by reading from a manuscript? I recommend moving increasingly away from merely reading words off a page. At the same time, I recommend writing a manuscript of the sermon as part of the preparation process. Why?

Manuscript writing gives the preacher opportunity to carefully think through the shaping of the message. With the contemporary blessing of word processing, blocks of manuscript material may be sequenced, rearranged, and edited to help the message hang together.

Manuscript writing disciplines the choice of words and phrases, which may otherwise be left to the inspiration of the delivery moment. Manuscript writing helps ensure that language is for an oral, rather than a written, end product. (We will think more about that when we consider the use of language in preaching.)

Putting it down in manuscript form also provides a foundation for producing whatever paper prompts the preacher will use to deliver the message. These may be highlighting key words or phrases, complete or basic notes, or a list of words prompting the preacher's memory.

Preparing a manuscript helps the speaker remember that people have a ten-minute attention span. Having to write a manuscript spurs the preacher to plan reengagement of listeners.

Some preachers have the gift or skill and/or significant experience in speaking extemporaneously. Most preaching can be improved by the discipline of at least frequent manuscript writing. I recommend it!

But back to the central task of structuring a message.

Factors Involved in Shaping the Sermon

The central theme. Shaping facilitates the effective communication of the sermon's big idea. Shaping enables the sermon to hang together around this big idea. Thus, without a clearly focused big idea, the structure of a message and thus its unity suffers. If the big idea is clear and well focused, the preacher is a long way toward effective structuring.

Literary genre of the passage. I used to offer messages from every part of the Bible with the same three-pronged fork. I have, however, come to the conviction that not all biblical genres should be preached the same way. For example, psalm and story are different literary genres than epistle. Psalm preaching should structure around painting the ancient poet's word pictures. The plotline of a story can effectively provide the structure for shaping a message. Especially in Paul's epistles, the message is often in the argument. That has a major impact on how to shape the sermon. Consider the literary genre of the passage as you come to shape or structure a message.

Purpose of the message. Fourth-century, St. Augustine, drawing on principles of ancient rhetoric, said that sermons have one or a combination of the following purposes, to teach, to delight, to persuade.

> ➤ To teach: This purpose for preaching is information. It tends to deal mostly with the content of faith. The preacher needs to ask, Is this going to be a teaching message?

> To delight: This purpose aims at inspiring. It centers in appeal to the imagination. The preacher asks, Is my purpose here to inspire, comfort, encourage?
> To persuade: This moves hearers to action. It opens up ethical responses in listeners' everyday lives. The preacher asks, Is my purpose to motivate to action?

A message may have more than one of these, but an over-riding purpose will probably be present. And that over-riding purpose will influence how the preacher structures the message. For example, a message focused on teaching doctrine is more likely to be structured deductively and propositionally.

Shaping a sermon may be through deduction or induction or a combination of the two. Because deduction or induction or both is crucial for shaping a sermon, let me go into greater detail here.

Deductive Processing

The shaping of a sermon moves from general idea to specifics, from theme to particulars. Deductive processing tends to be linear. It usually includes a series of specific statements or propositions which develop or grow out of the big idea This is the classic form of Western preaching, i.e., "three points and a poem!"

Deductive messages may be effectively shaped around contrast, *Not this, but this.*

For example, consider a message based in Jesus' parable of the Pharisee and the Tax Collector. (Luke 18:9-14). The big idea may be this: God looks for humility rather than self righteousness in those who approach God. The structure of the message may very simply be:

> Not this—the self-righteous tax collector
> But this—the mercy-seeking sinner

Deductive messages may also be shaped around a question. The outline then becomes a series of applications. A common question is, if so, what then?

For example, here's a message based in the story of Cornelius in Acts 10 and 11. The big idea drawn from this story might be, Christ's followers need to experience conversion to God's loving openness to all people everywhere. The responses to, "if so, what then" might be the following:

- We need to recognize our own need for ongoing conversion.
- We need to respond to the converting impact of key encounters.
- We need to relate to people not with upfront judgment, but upfront openness to what God may be doing in their lives.

Effective outlines for a deductive format exhibit the following characteristics:

- Unity: All main points of the outline grow out of and are linked to the big idea. Unity in an outline is enhanced by the use of parallel statements. Some preachers use alliteration to make an outline unified, clear, and memorable.
- Movement: The main points involve progression. Rather than circling like a plane looking for a place to land, the main points take listeners somewhere.
- Proportion: While not all points in the outline are necessarily the same in length, no one statement overwhelms or eclipses another.
- Climax: The strongest point in an outline should be the final statement. Never end with a "fizzle."

Two Illustrations of Deductive Shaping

"How Does God Speak to Us?" Psalm 19
(Long, 1989, p. 94)

    I) God speaks through nature. (1-6)
        A) In silent processes of life
        B) In cosmic wonder of universe

    II) God speaks through the divine Word. (7-11)
         A) In the Bible
         B) In preaching/teaching of God's people
    III) God speaks in our life experiences. (12-14)
         A) In our sense of failure and sin
         B) In our hunger to be faithful

"Wait!" Isaiah 40:27-31
(A drama in four acts or successive pictures)

    I)   The Human Problem
         A. God, you do not see.
         B. God, you allow injustice.
    II) God's response—gives a renewed vision of God.
    III) The condition—"wait" means
         A. Taking time for God.
         B. Trust in God's timing.
    IV) The Promise—soar, run, walk.

Inductive Processing

By contrast to deductive development, inductive presentations move from particulars to the general theme. Inductive preaching is more organic than linear. It may not have a clear and propositional outline. The big idea may become apparent later rather than earlier. Inductive structuring invites listeners on a journey involving experiences of their lives and moving toward a biblical theme. Inductive preaching helps listeners participate in the process of discovery.

Kenton Anderson suggests studying or preparing to preach inductively. To do this he offers the following "Steps to an Inductive Sermon"

    1. Start where the listener is. In other words, anticipate the listeners' problem or question.
    2. Clarify the question. "Inductive preachers need to take the listener's presenting problem and reshape it in the form of a research question—something that can be resolved through further investigation or experience."

3. Offer a solution. "The preacher leads the listener to a place of obedience and submission to the God who loves him or her and wants to bring healing."
4. Anticipate the future. "Induction takes a problem-solving approach to the sermon." (Anderson, 2006, p. 77f)

Here is a message based in the story of Hagar, primarily from Genesis 16:1-14. The big idea could be this, "God sees, loves, and wants to use unseen, cast-off, forsaken people." The following are thought-blocks moving toward the biblical story and this theme.

> Kid's games of peek-a-boo or hide-and-go-seek. Kids think they can't be seen.
>> Did you ever get lost as a child? Or did you have a child that was temporarily missing?
>>> Recent time spent downtown watching often unseen people—street people, those who slip on and off the bus.
>>>> People in Haiti tent villages or orphans of the world—seemingly forsaken.
>>>>> Have *we* ever felt forsaken, cast off like an old shirt? There is a story in the Bible about a woman whose name can mean "forsaken."
>> Retell the story of Hagar with backgrounds.
>>> Hagar was not forsaken by God, but is seen ("The God Who Sees" 16:13), loved, and used by God for God's purposes.
> Contemporary story of a person who felt forsaken, but was seen, loved, used by God.

Do you see the difference in approach and in shaping between deductive and inductive preaching? Both have their uses. We should be able to preach both deductively and inductively. Deductive preaching presumes authority. Inductive preaching seeks to gain authority by appeal to listener interest. Deductive preaching tells people what the preacher believes they need to know. Inductive preaching invites listeners on a journey with the preacher.

Combination of Inductive and Deductive

A practical and effective method of shaping a message is to combine the two. The preacher may begin inductively with several particulars or specifics which connect with listeners. These may be stories, current events, striking statements, experiences of the preacher or of the listeners. Between a third and half-way into the message, the preacher may move to the Scripture passage and the big idea. Continuing deductively, he may then identify applications of the big idea which are presented in a more linear fashion. In traditional terms, the inductive part of the sermon may be an extended introduction to the message, hooking the listeners' attention, seeking common ground, promising a solution to a problem, and orienting toward the Bible passage.

Such a message may flow as follows:
Particulars------Theme-------Particulars
(Induction)   (Deduction)

Many of the messages I have preached in recent years have taken this shape. Below is the general outline of one message based in John 2, titled, "What Happens When Jesus Shows Up?" The big idea is the answer to the question in the title, When Jesus shows up, He reveals His glory and confronts us with who He really is.

Recent Holy Land trip in which we passed through but didn't stop at Cana of Galilee—not an important place in Jesus' day or today.
In Jesus, God showed up in a common, Jewish neighborhood.
> Stories in the gospel of John about what happened when Jesus shows up in human situations.
> Retell the Cana story.
> What happened when Jesus showed up?

(Up to this point the message has developed inductively. It continues deductively.)
1. Jesus' presence reveals His glory (John 2:11).
   What is glory?
   What is the impact of glory in our everyday life?

(The Marriage Feast at Cana of Galilee is only one of the two, linked stories in John 2.)
2. Jesus' presence also confronts us with who He is
   (John 2:13 ff —The Cleansing of the Temple)
What will Jesus in our midst mean for us, either in a common, everyday setting or in centers of religious and political power?

Using the Shape of a Bible Narrative as Sermon Structure

When preaching from Bible narratives, an effective way to structure the message (and one which primarily proceeds inductively) uses the story's shape as the sermon's structure. Retell the ancient story in contemporary format and language.

As the plot unfolds, offer application. Or invite listeners to identify with characters in the story. Often, a contemporary story may be set alongside the ancient story. In a sermon on the story of Hannah and the birth of Samuel (1 Samuel 1), one of my students recently told the story of struggle with infertility experienced by him and his wife. The combination of ancient and contemporary story proved powerful.

Consider, for example, a story-oriented message based in John 8:2-11. Its big idea could be: Jesus graciously invites guilt-ridden people to a new way of life. The message invites listeners to identify with the various characters in the story.

> Here are the accusers—They think they are upholding the law.
> > Here is the woman—She is guilty and probably very angry at how she is being treated. Would there be yet another condemnation of her?
> > > Here is Jesus—He turns away the self-righteousness of religious leaders, declines to condemn the woman, but invites her to a new way of living.

Below are the broad contours of a message based in one of Jesus' parables found in Luke 19:11-27, titled "Successful or Faithful?"

The big idea is: Jesus calls us to be publicly faithful to the concerns of an absent King even though this faithfulness may not seem to bring immediate dividends.

"Once upon a time…" Briefly retell the parable in the form of a story with historical background. Jesus' hearers would have recognized that background.
    Link with the nearby story of Zachaeus.
       Back to the story Jesus told
- "Do business with these (funds) *until* and *because* I am coming back."
- "We do not want this man to rule over us." Will we be committed to the absent King whether or not it pays us now to do so? Contemporary illustration of faithfulness regardless of consequences.
- The servants' increase on their investment. Reward is more responsibility not more privilege.
- The servant who buried the money

State the big idea
- Apply to tithing
- Mother Theresa story

Restate the big idea

Homiletics professor, Thomas Long, urges variety in methods of shaping. "Whenever the gospel has been faithfully proclaimed, the intersection between the claims of the faith and the specific circumstances of the hearers has evoked suitable but ever-varying forms." (Long, 1989, p.105). Most of us will have a default structuring method depending on the way we think and process information. However, we benefit our preaching and our listeners by learning other ways of structuring sermons.

However we sequence materials in our sermons, let us insist that they hang together. Do not let the message suffer from inadequate shaping. As George Sweazey has observed, "Good structure does not make good preaching, but poor structure prevents it." (Sweazey, 1976, p.81).

Reflection

Consider how you might structure a sermon drawn from the following passages of varied literary genre.

Romans 12:1-2
Psalm 130
Exodus 3:1-15
Proverbs 3:3-10
Mark 4:1-20
Revelation 4:1-11

Chapter 7
Start with an Earthquake and Build to a Climax!

IT WAS A movie director's maxim, "Start with an earthquake and build to a climax!" Apply that to a sermon and you have something like, Start and end strong! Avoid fumbling at the beginning and fizzling at the end.

Start Strong!

Hook people in the first two minutes. The hook is something which connects with their life experiences and promises that giving you the next minutes will be worth their while. We cannot assume people have come with bated breath to hear what we have to say. So don't begin a sermon with, "My text is … Please turn to …" Don't begin with "Today, we're going to talk about Christian Perfection!" (or whatever doctrine is upfront in your denomination). Fred Craddock used to tell his students to assume their listeners almost didn't come to church that morning.

Sondra Willobee, a United Methodist pastor observes, "If we don't capture our hearers right away, they may drift off to daydream or doodle on the bulletin. Wary, distracted, sophisticated, or jaded, our listeners are harder than ever to reach" (Willobee, 2009, p. 11).

Kenton Anderson uses vivid imagery when he talks about the importance of effective introductions:

Starting immediately into detailed cognitive discussion is like trying to start your car when it is thirty degrees below zero. Or it is as if the people show at the airport to get on the plane, but you've already got it up to 25,000 feet. "Come on up," you say. "That's OK," they answer. "We'll see you when you come back down to earth."

—Anderson, 2006, p. 150

Get Attention

Attention-getting openings don't just happen. They are intentional. They are planned! In fact, a preacher may be looking for an attention-getting opening all week long. It's like a fisherman throwing out a line with a baited hook on the end of it. Don't assume attention. Capture attention.

One way to hook listeners' attention early is through conflict. Someone has said, "If you want someone's attention, start a fight" (old Irish proverb).

The Bible is full of conflict. There's Cain and Abel, Abraham and Lot, Jacob and Esau, Moses and Pharaoh, David and Goliath, Jesus and the Pharisees, Paul and Barnabas.

Good stories major in conflict, multiple conflicts. In fact, an English teacher declares, "In literature, only conflict is interesting" (Willobee, 2009, p.13). Why else would I and several other pastors I know thrive on murder mystery stories?

Jump in the Middle of Things

Leap into the middle of the action. You can fill in the gaps later. God breaks into the middle of our human routines. So should preachers!

Disclose and Withhold Information

"Marley was dead, to begin with." That's the way Dickens opens, *A Christmas Carol*. A comment that both discloses and withholds information raises questions and heightens interest.

Start with an Earthquake and
Build to a Climax!

Ask a Question

Questions are often-used and usually effective openings. In fact, asking questions all through a sermon is a good way to foster a dialogical tone.

Sometimes a first sentence question needs amplification. For example, I opened a message on Peter and Judas, who failed Jesus in the last week before the cross, with "Have you ever failed a friend?" I followed up that question with,

> We just weren't there for our friend when he or she needed us. We were careless and spoke or acted in a way that offended our friend. We didn't measure up to the friend's expectations of us. We failed a friend.

Or here's an example from an opening to a message based in one of Jesus' post-resurrection appearances. Key questions follow.

> John Crabtree was an Army veteran, wounded in Vietnam, on permanent disability. Crabtree had been steadily receiving benefits from the government.
>
> But one day, out of the blue, this VN vet received official notification from the government of his own death. Needless to say, this was quite a shock!
>
> Mr. Crabtree wrote the government stating that he was very much alive and would like to continue receiving his benefits. The letter did no good. Mr. Crabtree then tried calling the government. Have you ever tried to call the government? Phone calls didn't change the situation either. Finally, as a last resort, the veteran contacted a local television station, which ran a human-interest story about his situation. During the interview, the reporter asked him, "How do you feel about this whole ordeal?" The veteran chuckled and said, "Well, I feel a little frustrated by it," he admitted. "After all," Crabtree continued, "have you ever tried to prove that you're alive?"

Have you ever tried to prove that you're alive?

Sketching a Vivid Character or Painting a Picture

I began a message on "A Compelling Vision" by reflecting on the nearby Vancouver Winter Olympics which had glued folks to their TVs.

> We've been through days of watching Olympic athletes in nearby Vancouver and Whistler. We have watched them in the agony of defeat and ecstasy of victory.
>
> We have watched faces filled with emotion standing on the medal podium during their national anthems. We have watched skiers go into endless free falls and skaters take embarrassing tumbles. Can you imagine what it's like to fall on your face in front of millions of people and then have the scene replayed a dozen times! We saw a Canadian figure skater compete just two days after her mother died of a heart attack and we felt her deep emotion. For all of these athletes there is a compelling vision which drives them.

Or here's an attempt to pull people into the amazing imagery of Ezekiel 37's Valley of Dry Bones:

> Pastor Ezekiel might have succeeded well in Hollywood. Well, maybe not Hollywood, but Pastor Ezekiel sees things in vivid pictures. Pastor Zeke sees visions in Technicolor, hears God in Dolby Sound. Ezekiel 37 would make an amazing scene from a movie. Can't you just see it? Bones! Very many, very dry! Bones everywhere! And here's this kind of weird preacher, preaching to the dead, dry bones. You know, sometimes preaching may not kill, but it can put folks to sleep. And don't go telling me you never go to sleep on *my* preaching!

Striking Statement

Sometimes we can gain attention quickly by a striking statement. Preaching at a seminary graduation ceremony, I began by pondering whether or not I should delve into popular culture and expound on the meaning of a bumper sticker I saw on the way to the event. "Atheists make better lovers!" Then I added, "Now what are the theological implications of that?"

Humor

No, starting every sermon with a joke isn't necessary, would become repetitious, and would exhaust most of our joke collection. We also have to beware lest our sense of humor needlessly offend and lose listeners before we even begin. I did that recently with what I thought was an OK ethnic joke. I was told that a new family checking out our church left offended.

On the other hand humor connects. Our denominational conference leader began a sermon by telling how twice in one day he had sliced the electric cord for his hedge clippers. When a leader pokes fun at himself, people connect with him. I began a Palm Sunday message with this:

> A six-year-old comes home from Palm Sunday services proudly carrying his palm branch. Mom and Dad quiz him on his Sunday school lesson for the day. He responds enthusiastically, "Jesus came to Jerusalem on a donkey. And the happy people waved their palm branches and sang, O Suzanna ..."

Strong beginnings acquire attention. And without listeners' attention, a sermon is an exercise in irrelevance.

Promise

But strong beginnings also offer promise. Strong introductions promise that giving you their attention for next minutes it will be worth while for listeners. To do that, the preacher will need to make the case quickly that what he or she has to say has something to do with where listeners live.

At the same time, warns Thomas Long, preachers should not promise more than they can fulfill.

> Often preachers, usually in well-intentioned attempts to begin sermons in an exciting fashion, generate sparkling, ear-catching,

> arresting, even glitzy introductions. Such introductions undoubtedly intrigue the hearers, but they also make promises to the hearers that go unfulfilled....The preacher says, "Listen! Listen! You are going to hear a great sermon." But after a few deceptive beginnings, when there was nothing of substance to follow, the crowd learns not to pay any attention.
> —Long, 1989, p. 141

Here's the opening of a Thanksgiving Sunday sermon on Lamentations 3:19-24 entitled "Gratitude in the Light and in the Dark":

> This week most of us will gather with families and friends to celebrate Thanksgiving. We will express our gratitude by eating up as much of God's creation as possible in one sitting. Between overdosing on turkey and pumpkin pie, we will remember to "count our blessings." We will remember the good things in our lives and be grateful for them. Most images of Thanksgiving are full of light and gladness. In fact, the entire Hallowthankmas season is one which is supposed to be celebrative. However, maybe it's a difficult season for some. Some may have family members in harm's way in Iraq or Afghanistan. Some may have recently lost a love or loved one. Some may be dealing with a difficult diagnosis for yourself or someone close to you. Some may be reeling from failure. First quarter at SPU may have been tough. Some may feel very much alone. Some may feel in darkness. Can we give thanks in the darkness?

Included in the introduction's offer of promise may be that the preacher will shed light on an important biblical theme and/or passage. Traditionally introductions were expected to provide orientation toward the exposition of the text. For example here is an early paragraph in a message titled "Called to Follow Jesus:"

> "Don't follow me; follow my teachings." That's what the great Buddha once said to his followers. Buddhism is about the teachings of the Buddha. That is a huge difference with Christianity. What Jesus taught *is* important. But most of all Jesus called people to follow Him. Jesus would *not* say, "Don't follow me; follow my

teachings." Who Jesus is and our relationship with Him is at the core of our faith. In fact, instead of being called "Christian," I would rather be known as a "Christ-follower." This morning we think together about what it means to be called to follow Jesus.

Listen once more to Sondra Willobee:

A well-constructed hook is a form of pastoral care. We pay our parishioners the courtesy of engaging their attention before speaking of difficult matters. We honor them when we respect the fears, doubts, fatigue, or rebellion that almost kept them from worship. A good hook meets our congregations in their need and prepares them to go the next step of the sermon with us.
—Willobee, 2009, p. 26

Conclude Strong and in a Timely Manner

A sermon's other bookend is its conclusion. When it is time to close the sermon, don't just circle aimlessly looking for a place to land. Set the aircraft down strongly and in a timely manner.

Martin Luther is reported to have advised, "When you see your hearers most attentive, then conclude." Listeners often have a sense of when a sermon is really over. But preachers may keep on preaching. My recommendation is, Quit sooner than later. When the sermon is over, stop.

Some preachers see an evangelistic conclusion as inevitable and required. Thus, regardless of the purpose and aim of the message, they move toward a "commitment for Christ" conclusion. I suggest that while all sermons should involve an invitation or challenge to response, not all must lead to an "altar call." On the other hand, some sermons fizzle rather than finish. The ending does not drive home the message or leave listeners with work to do on their own.

But how to conclude a sermon? How to set the plane down when everyone knows it's time to land? How to conclude depends largely on what the sermon aims to do. Is its primary goal, in Augustine's terms, to instruct, inspire, or persuade?

Here are some kinds of conclusions.

Summarize

If a sermon's purpose is to instruct, a preacher may conclude by reiterating the main points he wants listeners to carry away with them. The conclusion may tie loose ends together. However, it is not just a recap, but contains application. "Conclusions," says Rick Warren, "are more than summaries. It's where you challenge your church to apply your message" (Warren, 2007).

Challenge to Act

While appropriate for any message, a challenge applies especially to persuasive sermons. There are people in our congregations who respond well to "homework," short lists of things the preacher asks them to do as a result of the message.

Story

A conclusion may use a story which drives the theme home. Most of us will not find a memorable story with which to conclude every message. But a real-life story which illustrates the message can create a powerful conclusion. But beware of telling the story, then driving it home with heavy-handed exhortations. Let the Spirit work through the story.

Here's a conclusion to a message on Mary, Mother of Jesus, titled, "A Girl God Used."

> Did you read the Christmas Day feature in the *Seattle Times* about a reporter injured in an accident and stuck in an Iowa snow drift a couple years ago?
>
> At the hospital Dan Simmons encountered a remarkably helpful nurse. After Dan was treated, Deb Hamilton and her husband drove him 100 plus miles to St. Paul, MN, where he could catch a flight to San Diego. That's beyond the call of duty for a hospital nurse!

Start with an Earthquake and Build to a Climax!

> Deb Hamilton emailed Dan Simmons' mother, "Bob and I feel honored to have been chosen by the Lord that night to do His work and help Him by helping one of His children."

The conclusion may be a place to tell how this sermon impacts you, the preacher. How has the Spirit spoken to you as you have prepared this message? Maybe, the concluding story can be your own story.

Series of Questions

Many preachers conclude with a series of questions. Questions may be a more engaging way to invite commitment and response than direct exhortations. A question or series of questions may continue the inductive or discovery process.

- What impact does this insight have on my journey?
- Are we willing to say yes to what Jesus is saying to us?
- This week to what one thing is Jesus calling me in response to what I've heard?
- How might this word make a difference in how I live today and tomorrow?
- Will I leave today with hope rather than fear?

Here's another part of the conclusion to "A Girl God Used" cited above. The series of questions combined with a story to conclude strongly.

> So what might this mean when the rubber meets the road of our lives? *God wants to use us as God's instruments.* No, it will probably not be through virgin birth or something quite so dramatic.
> But how about influencing my surroundings for God?
> How about raising my children to be people who love and know God?
> How about, as one grandmother told me last Sunday, being consumed with prayer for her children and grandchildren?

How about being a fully devoted follower of Jesus?
Some Protestants have begun to view Mary as Jesus' first disciple. What a privilege that is! How about following in her footsteps?

A Surprise or Abrupt Ending

Rick Warren suggests that "the best conclusions sneak up on congregations rather than being obvious and expected." (Warren, 2007)

Though it was a few years ago, I still remember the impact of a sudden conclusion by the preacher at First Baptist Church in Vancouver, BC. At the end of a message about following Jesus and bearing His cross, the preacher picked up a length of wood, held it on his shoulder as though the cross-piece of a cross, and then sat down. The congregation sat in stunned silence for a few moments. Even the worship team members were caught off guard taking time to make their way to the front for a closing song.

One homiletics professor recommended, "Conclude your sermons like a player piano." The old player piano, he observed, "went lickety bang, then all of a sudden stopped. Just like that! The piece finished, the music quit! And that is the way to stop a sermon" (Demaray, 1990, p. 130).

Conclude strongly and before people have turned you off. Let the conclusion be with emotional intensity, but not heavy-handed. "I count a sermon a success," said one parishioner, "if I think about it again during the week." Modest standard, maybe, but probably realistic.

Reflection

1. Think of a sermon you heard most recently.
2. What kind of beginning did the preacher use? Did it work in getting your attention and promising something worthwhile in the message?
3. How did the preacher conclude? Was the conclusion overdue? Did the sermon finish strong?

Chapter 8
Language Fit to Be Spoken

SOME PREACHERS SEEM to think authenticity requires us to use the first words that come to mind. "Being concerned about word choices is so technical. Preaching is spiritual work." So certain preachers think (even if they may not say so out loud). But words are the tool chest of a communicator. Why use an axe when a chisel will do better?

Someone has appropriately asked preachers, "Are your sermons pea soup?" Pea soup isn't just what you put in a bowl. Pea soup is also what aviator's call thick fog that makes simple landings complicated. Pea soup preaching results when language is poorly chosen. Pea soup results when preachers listen to themselves on CD and are not quite sure what they mean. Pea soup results when the preacher's vocabulary is significantly beyond that of the listeners. Are our sermons pea soup?

Or, consider the image offered by Fred Craddock:

> Any preacher who does not take time to develop for himself some grasp of the nature and meaning of words ... will soon fall silent, frustrated, disenchanted, weary of the sound of his own voice, and convinced that what descended on him was not a dove, but an albatross.
>
> —Craddock, 2001

Some of us are good with words. We have "the gift of gab." Others struggle with verbal fluency. All preachers benefit by giving significant thought to the choice of words and phrases. After all, we are in the business of communicating for God. And words are vehicles for communication.

Here is a principle for using words in communication: Never underestimate the intelligence of a congregation, but never overestimate its vocabulary.

Graduates from a theological school have a vocabulary of about 12,000 words. Compare that to the average congregation member's vocabulary of about 7,500 words. Remove 2,000 technical words and 500 local expressions. Thus, the language of preaching should be basically the common, shared vocabulary of a congregation, 5,000 words. Most newspapers are written at about the tenth-grade level in order to avoid missing major portions of their audiences.

This eliminates "the language of Canaan" or, "Christianese" words and phrases known to those brought up in the church, but unrecognized by an increasingly biblically illiterate society. This also cuts down on theological terms and ten-dollar multi-syllabic words—impressive in research papers, but not useful in oral communication, and especially in sermons. Trimming down removes most abstract words as well. Instead the preacher will choose words that are concrete, that earth reality in the senses.

Poet and insightful author, Kathleen Norris, talks about "incarnational language." She means, "ordinary words that resonate with the senses as they aim for the stars" (Willobee, 2009, p. 90). The Bible is full of sensory images. Jesus was master of the sensory image. "Consider the lilies of the field"; "You are the salt of the earth." In the twenty-first century, our preaching words should do the same but with words and images out of our time and place.

Here is the bottom line regarding the words we use to say well what we have to say, Preachers work toward a clear, concrete oral style even when writing a manuscript.

Oral Style Versus Written Style

To respond to this important question, remember that in the language of oral communication, the pace is set by the speaker. Orally, punctuation is indicated only by the voice. Paragraphs and outline are not as clear as they are in writing. Grammar is important, but not as important as in written communication. Until words are spoken, the experience is incomplete in contrast to the written finished product.

Simple Sentences Simple Words

Oral versus written language involves the above three elements. "Every word that can be spared should be cut out" (Sweazey, 1976). Out of another era, Beecher advised, "Don't whip with a switch that has leaves on if you want to tingle."

Creative preacher and writer, Calvin Miller urges:

> When we finish a sermon, we must go through it sentence by sentence, replacing weak words with those that are robust. Each of the sermon's key words individually must sing ... For instance, the word "break" is okay. The word "burst" may be better. The word "blast" may be best.
>
> —Miller, 1989, p. 113

Miller continues with illustrations, borrowed from wordsmith preacher, Peter Marshall:

> "The roar of the siren" over "the alarm."
> "He blistered them with words" versus "He criticized them severely."
> "We disguise death with flowers" versus "We avoid thinking of death."
> "The cold stone slab" versus "The spot where Jesus' lay."

Word Selection Principles

➢ Major in one- or two-syllable words. You'll be amazed at how powerful short words can be!

- Major in strong words, that is, nouns and verbs rather than modifiers.
- Usually repeat nouns rather than opting for pronouns. With pronouns, listeners may lose track of whom or what the antecedents are.
- To convey immediacy and directness, use active voice rather than passive voice as often as possible. In active voice, the subject performs the action. For example,

  - Active: "Everyone had a good time."
  - Passive: "A good time was had by all."
  - Active: "Shakespeare wrote a play"
  - Passive: "A play was written by Shakespeare"

- Break up complex sentences into simple sentence units. J. I. Packer and N.T. Wright can successfully bring complex oral sentences to appropriate conclusions. Let them! They are the exception rather than the norm.
- Break up long paragraphs into one or two sentence units.
- After finishing a draft of a sermon manuscript, go over it, requiring yourself to break up sentences and paragraphs into simple, orally accessible units.
- Use concrete versus abstract words and phrases.
- Someone suggests a "ladder of abstraction." This ladder begins with Bessie, a real cow. Up the ladder toward increasing abstractness is cow, livestock, farm assets, assets, wealth. "Bessie" is the most interesting item on the ladder. Feature "Bessie" not a "farm asset."
- Be conversational. In other words, be personal, yourself, not artificial. A preacher should not talk at but with hearers.
- Major in first person rather than second person pronouns. Use "we" not "you." Why? "We" identifies with hearers rather than talking at or down to them.
- Major in words and images drawn from the experience of the hearers.

- Pile up questions. They give people something to think about. One way to develop an idea is to pepper it with questions. They give a dialogical tone and slip under defenses. They enable people at different stages to apply the message to them.
- Most often use present tense for narration. Present tense brings immediacy into the story.
- As Calvin Miller urges in the quotation above, prune needless, abstract, complex, and/or weak words from your rough draft.

Formatting a Sermon Manuscript

While we are talking about words, let me offer a suggestion for formatting. Format it for the eyes of the preacher not just the eyes of a reader. Fitting a sermon for oral delivery helps us deliver a sermon. Remember a sermon manuscript is not a research paper, but background for an oral presentation.

Let me tell you what I do to format a sermon manuscript so it is useful in delivery:

- I rigorously break up the long paragraphs. I use one-sentence paragraphs which are run down the page, assisting the eye when I look down during delivery.
- I opt for half-sheet print-outs rather than full pages.
- I use at least fourteen-point font. OK, your younger eyes may work better than mine! But facilitate delivery by how you format your papers.
- I highlight key words and phrases I want to stand out when I glance toward the paper on the pulpit or lectern.

Verbal Signposting

Before leaving verbal, word-choice aspects of a message, let me offer suggestions regarding what I call "verbal signposting." Verbal signposts are connectors between segments of the message. These help listeners, who do not have a sermon manuscript in hand, to follow the train of the preacher's thought. Sometimes PowerPoint outlines offer clues to the movement of a message. But even with PowerPoint, preachers should plan for verbal cues. "What we are trying to accomplish in the connective moments of a sermon is to provide enough guidance to the hearers to ensure that they are following the movement of the sermon" (Long, p. 150).

Verbal signposts may:

- Point to the opening of a new idea, "To begin with …"
- Move to the next point, "We've been observing …" "Now look with me …"
- Signal a conclusion, "Finally …," "In conclusion …"

I suggest avoiding, "My first point is …" which sounds too pedantic. Try something like "What I hope you hear first is …" "Here's a second picture I hope we carry away with us today …"

Verbal signposts are useful when leading into or out of a quotation. They may be nothing more than, "A famous preacher once said …"

In conclusion, one benefit of manuscript writing is that we train ourselves to be intentional in our choices of words and phrases. If we need a further nudge in the direction of this discipline, here's a word from homiletics professor Robert Hoch:

> Getting into the habit of having a full manuscript for the sermon helps to push us to think about the message in advance of the pressure to go out and buy a homiletical version of the *Saturday Night Special*.
>
> —Hoch, 2008, p. 26

Reflection

1. Work with at least a page of a recent message you delivered or from someone else's sermon.
2. Is the language oral as described above? Does it connect with the ear as well as with the eye?

3. Watch for long sentences and paragraphs. Fix them!
4. Watch for words that do not grip or are too long or too abstract or too theologically obtuse. Fix them!
5. How can you practice speaking and writing in ways that will enhance your oral use of language?

Chapter 9
Glow Over It

IS A SERMON ready to be delivered simply because we have completed a manuscript of what we want to say? Usually not! Four questions about the manuscript in hand help a preacher assess what he or she has prepared:

1. Is it clear? In other words, have I focused on one "big idea?"
2. Is it coherent? Does the message hold together?
3. Is it concrete? Have I earthed ideas and concepts so that listeners can touch, smell, and see, not just hear what I have to say?
4. Is it climactic? Does this message build toward its conclusion and does it have urgency?

Is a sermon ready? Ask these questions. Sometimes they will send us back both to our knees and to our word processors to continue the work of preparing to deliver a message. But if and when the preacher is convinced the sermon is ready or at least as ready as it will ever get, then we need to heed William Sangster's advice "Glow over it!" Sangster was a British Methodist, a master preacher of the mid-twentieth century. In his little book, *Power in Preaching,* Sangster wrote this:

> Some preaching fails in power because it fails in passion. It may be intellectually respectable ... but there is no glow about it. The people depart but they are inwardly unmoved, and they are unmoved because the preacher himself was unmoved. No one can carry conviction to others who is not filled with conviction himself ... A man who is not moved himself has little hope of moving others.
>
> —Sangster, 1958, pp 89-91

Sangster admits that he's talking about feelings, emotions, something that will be expressed differently by different preachers. But Sangster urges, "Let the feeling show itself how it will; but if there is no feeling, the preaching will fail in conviction and all the preacher's words be lost on the wind."

So how did Sangster urge preachers to glow over it? How does passion come into preaching? "Prayer is the chief way," writes Sangster. He cites an African American preacher who said that in preparation to preach he "read himself full" and "thought himself clear" and "prayed himself hot" (Sangster, 1958, p. 92).

The entire preaching preparation process requires ongoing prayer. But the kind of prayer preparation Sangster is talking about needs to happen especially on Sunday morning, requiring that we get to church early before the hurricane of other things envelopes us. Before I engaged in "the ministry of checking," that is making sure everything was ready for the services of the morning, I found I had to prayerfully go over the message one more time.

Preachers who prayerfully go over what they have to say find that the message becomes a part of them. Then, use of a manuscript or notes will not just be reading words off a page. Rather, it will be communication from the speaker's heart and mind to the listeners.

As Sangster describes "glowing over it," he takes us back before the sermon was envisioned to the life of the preacher. He observes, "Anything which deepens a preacher's faith in preaching adds to his passion in preaching the Word."

Sangster urges, "As he (or she) prepares ... let him (or her) hold steadily in mind that through the medium of his sermon the Holy

Glow Over It

Spirit may work a miracle of transformation in someone's life, and the thought of it and the hope of it will kindle ... expectation." Remember the person whom God changed through the preached word. Keep that person in mind. My copy of Sangster's book belonged to my father, who here penciled in this prayer, "Do it again, Lord!"

Sangster went on to say, "Anything which militates against familiarity in handling the word will also help to keep the glow in preaching." "The preacher," says Sangster about the sermon ready to be delivered, "must feel its freshness again and give it with the dew upon it."

Finally, this master preacher urges us, "Realizing that power in preaching comes from the Spirit/Wind of God, we can put up our sail." (Sangster, 1958, p. 93).

Often on Sunday mornings I have prayed something like this, *"O God, let this sermon be like the framework built to hold a section of concrete sidewalk. The framework now awaits the pouring in of your Spirit. Please do not let your people be disappointed in hearing just from me, but let them hear from You!"*

When we think of what we need as we move from preparation to delivery, an old word may be as good as any. Unction is a word our preaching forebears used, but most of us have stopped using. Unction is what God does through us and sometimes in spite of us. "Unction," writes Sangster, "is that mystic plus in preaching which no one can define and no one with any spiritual sensitivity at all can mistake ... It is a thing apart from good sermon outlines, helpful spiritual insights, wise understanding, or eloquent speech. It can use all these media—and dispense with them. It is rare, indefinable, and unspeakably precious" (Sangster, 1958, p. 109f).

Maybe a vehicle for "unction" is the preacher's engagement in worship with the congregation before the sermon is delivered. Preaching functions best when it is in the context of worship. That is so with those who hear the sermon. It is also true with the one who delivers the sermon. The preacher, usually the pastor, needs to be the lead worshiper, not necessarily always upfront, but modeling worship as the service moves toward the time when the sermon is delivered. This means the service's organization or choreography will need to be planned ahead and/or delegated to someone else besides the one preaching. The preacher needs to be a worshiper if he or she is to preach with "unction."

I urge us to do the best we can, with all the resources at our disposal, to have something biblical and from God to say, and prepare to say it as well as we can. But then, we have to trust God to use what we place in His Hands. "God decided," wrote Paul to the Corinthians, "through the foolishness of our proclamation to save those who believe" (1 Corinthians 1:21).

Recognizing that preaching is not just our work, but a work of God's Spirit means that we "glow over it" during the entire preparation process, but especially during those hours and minutes before the sermon is to be delivered.

Reflection

1. Think back to the last time you preached.
2. Did you arrive early enough to "glow over" the sermon to be delivered?
3. Did you avoid becoming needlessly entangled with issues and problems in the hour before preaching?
4. Did you participate wholeheartedly with the congregation in worship?
5. If not, what can you do differently the next time you are given the privilege and responsibility of preaching?

Chapter 10
Deliver that Baby!

WHEN I SPEAK with couples in preparation for marriage, I often remind the man that he and I do not conceive and give birth to babies. She's the one who will deal with having babies. Thus, she is the one who primarily needs to be ready when the couple considers when and if to have a child. I have also watched women react negatively to men tritely using birth metaphors. So with apologies to those who actually do have babies, I suggest that preparation to preach is a little like gestation. Over hours and days, maybe even weeks, this seemingly living thing is growing and developing within your mind and heart. The act of preaching is a little like delivering that baby.

I was invited into a birthing room to spend a few moments with a mother who was by herself at this traumatic time. Between contractions she gasped, "Nobody ever told me this would be so hard!" With some preachers, the delivery of a sermon is relatively straightforward, even painless. Maybe that is why many books on preaching do not deal significantly with delivery. With some preachers, preparation is not so hard. But delivery is! Standing in front of people and proclaiming what you have prepared in the privacy of study and meditation may even be painful.

When we have something to say that is from God and out of God's Word, we want to say it well. We want what we have to say to connect and impact. Part of "saying it well" is preparing ourselves and our message. But key to "saying it well" is actually speaking the words so that the message in fact connects and communicates.

Effective delivery is not just learning *what to do*—positive techniques of public speaking—though these techniques are valuable. Effective delivery is also learning *what not to do*—avoiding that which distracts and serves as a barrier to communication. Victorian prince of preachers, Charles Spurgeon warned his students against what he called "ore rotundo." This Spurgeon defined as "that dignified, doctorial, inflated, bombastic style" (Spurgeon, undated, p. 119). We would call this "the stained-glass voice."

As often, Spurgeon delivered a particularly pungent illustration of what he thought preachers should not do.

> When a reverend gentleman was once blowing off steam in this way, a man in the aisle said he thought the preacher "had swallowed a dumpling," but another whispered, "No, Jack, he ain't swaller'd un; he's got un in his mouth a-wobbling."
> —Spurgeon, undated, p. 120

John Wesley, eighteenth century mentor of Methodists, taught his preachers by describing the kind of voice they should avoid.

> Some have a ... squeaking tone; some a singing or canting one; some an high, swelling, theatrical tone, laying too much emphasis on every sentence; some have an awful, solemn tone; others an odd, whimsical, whining one, not to be expressed in words.
> —Demaray, 1990, p. 157

Rather than fixating only on what we should not do, let me offer positive perspectives on what will be assets to sermon delivery.

Intensity or Passion

What is passion in preaching? It's not just vehemence or volume. Passion is the clear communication that what the preacher is saying matters to him or her. It communicates: "The message I am preaching is a big deal!" If it's not a big deal to the preacher, why should it be to the listener?

How we communicate passion depends on our personality. We should not be someone else in the pulpit than we are the rest of the time. However, we must "get into" the sermon. We must communicate that this message matters to us and to God.

Passion in preaching cannot be successfully faked. If something is not that important to the preacher, no technique of delivery will counteract lack of passion. The preacher is not acting a part or playing a role, but delivering huge good news to people who desperately need to hear it.

Passion in preaching is expressed in how we use our voice and our whole body. We will consider those aspects in a moment. But first, please hear me! Be intense about what you have to say in a way that fits who you are. Let this sermon come from deep inside you almost as if it were a baby to whom you are giving birth.

- Pray over it.
- Listen to the message yourself.
- Go over the message as if you were actually preaching it several times.
- Let go! Not totally maybe. Some preachers need restraint. But let go!
- Work at it! Communication is work. You should be tired when the sermon is over.

Voice

Haddon Robinson describes vocal issues in terms of pitch, punch, progress, and pause (Robinson, 1980, p 204 f). I suggest two more P's—Project! Pronounce!

Pitch involves voice inflection up or down. Vary pitch, but avoid the singsong approach. Vary pitch naturally. Listen to yourself on tape and see if you fit the singsong pattern. (Wait till the Tuesday after Sunday's sermon!)

A frequent stereotype is that lower-pitched voices are more authoritative. Women, in particular, and men with higher-pitched voices, may want deliberately to lower their pitch when they speak in public.

Punch is vocal emphasis. This may be done by volume, either louder or more toward an intense whisper. Punch communicates passion.

I will never forget attending a national gathering of preachers held in a large arena. For days great preachers thundered at us. But then, Max Lucado got up to speak. This well-known preacher and author held us spellbound by the power of words. There was punch, but it wasn't all volume.

Punch is most effective when it is periodic and emphasizes a point in the message. If the whole message is punched, it loses its impact.

Progress is the pace of vocal delivery. While some preachers would do well to slow down, I suggest that the greater danger is too slow a rate of delivery. The average rate of speech for English-speaking Westerners is 150 words per minute. But the average rate of comprehension is over three times greater than the average rate of speech. Consider this from a preaching-pastor,

> At 150 WPM or less, our listeners' brains have a surplus of time; time to daydream, time to doodle, time to disengage ... Slower discourses lend themselves to audience distraction and boredom."
> —Miller, 2003, p. 23

Pause serves as the punctuation marks of speech. According to Robinson, "The skilled speaker recognizes that pauses serve as commas, semicolons, periods, and exclamation points" (Robinson, 1980, p. 206). During much of my ministry, I have been afraid of pauses lest I lose people's attention. But I have increasingly observed how effective well-placed pauses can be. Pauses seldom seem as long to listeners as they do to the speaker.

But while affirming pauses, beware "vocalized pauses." This is when the preacher's voice continues even while he or she is not saying anything. "Um, er, you know, etc." may be unavoidable and acceptable in personal conversation, but need to be minimized in public communication. I have known students who thought it was helpful to count the number of "ums" in a fellow student's message.

Project. During her later years, I listened to preaching through my mother's ears. "I just can't hear what he is saying," Mother used to offer as an excuse for staying home on Sunday mornings. OK, the PA system should prevent the preacher from being inaudible. However, even the best PA will not compensate for a preacher who does not speak up. Even with the latest technology, preachers should speak to the back of the room.

Pronounce is the final P. This is another word for enunciate. A key factor here is the simple process of opening our mouths instead of speaking through our teeth. Try putting a pencil between your teeth and speaking around it. Open your mouth when you preach!

Skilled vocal musicians go to great lengths to ensure that words are understood. Why shouldn't preachers do the same? "Too artificial!" someone says. But do we want to be understood or not?

Accents may or may not hinder comprehension. Ask honest listeners if they can understand you. Remember the big issue is not "being yourself" but being understood.

Our Bodies

The delivery of a sermon involves passion, voice, and our bodies. Studies indicate that thirty-five percent of what we comprehend comes through words alone. Listeners receive sixty-five percent of our message by means other than words. Preaching is whole-person communication. Nonverbal communication is the way our whole bodies serve to deliver the message.

Appearance is one nonverbal factor. How we dress and how we are groomed says a lot about ourselves and about what we think of our audience. Are there wide social and cultural variances in how people expect a preacher to dress? Of course! And the preacher ought to respond to these expectations. For years I resisted adjusting my attire between sanctuary and gym services. But I finally realized that being the only person in the room with a coat and tie made a statement I did not want to make.

Gestures are huge nonverbal factors in communication. Haddon Robinson observes, "God designed the human body to move. If a congregation wants to look at a statue, they can go to a museum" (Robinson, 1980, p. 198). A preacher needs to learn to let his or her body speak.

Gestures are a natural part of most people's conversation. They hold interest and can also put the speaker at ease. I urge students who tend to be nervous, stiff, and rigid to find ways to loosen up their arms early in the message. Loosening their arms helps speakers relax and begin using their arms and hands normally. Also beware the hand-washing movement which communicates nerves not harnessed and under control.

Body movement that communicates effectively is natural, that is, spontaneous and does not call attention to itself. It is appropriate to content and context. For example, I gesture less at a funeral or memorial service. Good body movements are varied. Repetition of a single movement calls attention to itself, does not facilitate communication, and may actually lead to parodies.

Preaching space did not used to be a big issue. Preachers were expected to plant themselves behind the pulpit and deliver their message from there. Many still do so. But many do not! In fact, high-profile preachers often roam the front and occasionally get right down in people's faces.

How a preacher physically fills the space depends a great deal on personality. Bill Hybels of Willow Creek is mostly planted behind a lectern. John Maxwell roams dramatically. And the latter is sometimes held up as the model to emulate. However, no preacher should feel he or she must be like John Maxwell. Pacing may be distracting. On the other hand, leaving the pulpit occasionally may be an effective way to get attention and make a point.

A visiting preacher startled our relatively sedate sanctuary congregation by moving about the platform. Afterwards someone commented on how brave that was. I gently suggested that it wasn't an issue of courage, but of personality and habit.

Eye contact plays a huge role in communication. When I began preaching, it was not unusual for preachers to thunder at their congregations with their eyes fixed on the back wall of the sanctuary. I had a seminary professor who always looked about a foot over the heads of students. Some of us used to check out the back wall of his classroom, wondering what it was he saw there. Obviously, if that kind of impersonal communication ever worked in days gone by, it does not today. Today's listeners want to connect with the preacher. And one important way to connect is through the eyes of preacher and listener.

Two factors most often hinder good eye contact. One is being tied to our materials. Inability to move beyond merely reading words off a page dramatically reduces eye contact and therefore communication. Most people have only so much tolerance for being read to. If you have to start by reading a manuscript, do so. But work at preaching from the manuscript, not just reading it. Even before that, work toward producing oral materials that are easy to remember, easy to deliver. Long sentences require reading if we are to get them right. Look at listeners as much as and as often as you can.

While some preachers' eye contact is limited by being tied to their materials, other preachers are limited by *fear*. I know looking people in the eye can be scary! They may not be listening. Their reactions may not be what you hope for. Fear keeps us from looking listeners in the eye. Practice looking people in the eye in personal conversation as a prelude to visually connecting with preaching listeners.

For several years, I was privileged to have a well-known Bible teacher and commentator as a regular part of our congregation. While I did look his way periodically, I seldom saw his face. When

I did, I knew it was not a good signal. A compulsive note taker, he wrote down anything and everything he thought was worthwhile. If he was looking at me, I knew that in his mind I had ceased saying anything worthwhile.

Emotion in preaching must be addressed before leaving the sermon's delivery. A well-prepared sermon involves the emotions of the preacher from start to completion. The choice of words and materials influences whether or not hearers' emotions will be engaged. But at the point of the sermon's delivery, emotion can be a powerful communication factor—or emotion can be a manipulative device.

A classic Latin orator and teacher of rhetoric observed, "The principle essential for stirring the emotions of others is ... first to feel those emotions ourselves." Having something to say and saying it well involves the preacher's own emotions.

Someone has observed that "emotions are the highway for human motivation." We are seldom motivated by head or by heart, but by both. The question for preachers is whether or not our use of emotion is a healthy and vital part of communication or if it manipulates and is thus misused.

Common Misuses of Emotion

Emotions are misused if they are not combined with solid information. Effective and wise preachers lay an information base on which to make emotional appeals. While from another era, Charles Spurgeon is on target here.

> Rousing appeals to the affections are excellent, but if they are not backed up by instruction they are a mere flash in the pan, power consumed and no shot sent home. Rest assured that the most fervid revivalism will wear itself out in mere smoke, if it be not maintained by the fuel of teaching.
> —Spurgeon, undated, p. 73

Emotions are also used sloppily if fear and threat are not balanced by promise and faith. I once heard someone observe that "guilt is the method neurotic leaders use to keep neurotic followers in line." An African Bible School student recently tried to make the case with me that fear is a useful motivator for the pastor. However, the shelf life of guilt and fear motivation is not long even though the short-term impact may be strong. In the Bible, guilt is a natural and appropriate response to having offended our Divine Friend, but seldom a device used to get people to do what the leader/speaker wanted. Commandments are always in the context of covenant. And covenant is good news—promising, faith-fostering.

Listen to John Wesley, who claimed, "I live by preaching." Wesley urged early Methodist preachers, "If you cannot reason or persuade a man into the truth, never attempt to force him into it. If love will not compel him to come, leave him to God." Paul Chilcote comments on this statement by this eighteenth-century evangelist and preacher, "Scaring someone into saving faith was a strategy the Wesleys would not countenance." (Chilcote, 2004, p. 100).

In our day, fear mongering has become a commercially beneficial tactic. Scare people badly enough, and they will do what you tell them, at least in the short run. However, a major backlash against attempts to persuade based in fear and guilt has arisen. Many, particularly younger adults, have a low tolerance for being beaten over the head. Jesus came preaching "good news." Today's preaching, if it errs on one side should do so on the side of promise and faith.

Another way emotions are counterproductive is if the preacher's own emotions become the focus rather than the message. While congregations may be moved by emotional preaching, and while emotions are integral to persuasive preaching, the primary issue should not be the preacher's own intense emotion. The primary focus should always be on the message. People should not feel like they have to take care of the preacher and his or her emotions. At times effectively communicating a particularly moving message requires the preacher to rein in his emotions to avoid being distracting.

Counterproductive expression may not be merely the preacher breaking into tears, but also when he or she seems consumed by anger. Of course, an appropriate anger against evil and injustice is acceptable. But listeners should beware when a preacher seems particularly angry at someone or certain people. Some popular preachers today have made the "rant" into an art form. And yes, people often love to hear a speaker rant. But preaching is not the place for preachers to vent their anger.

Finally, emotions are misused when the preacher does not respect listeners' emotional thresholds. Because of their histories, many parishioners have thresholds which they are not comfortable allowing a preacher to pass. Those thresholds may involve space invasion (Don't get too close to me!) or emotional invasion (I can't stand graphic details of abuse or exploitation!). A preacher who exploits emotional vulnerability at a funeral or memorial service to offer an intense evangelistic appeal has probably unwisely crossed an emotional threshold. The impact is likely to be counterproductive, with listeners resisting the Gospel rather than responding positively.

Having offered warnings against misusing or exploiting emotions in preaching, let me return to the important place emotion does have in human motivation. Strong preaching does have an emotional appeal.

1. Strong preaching is set in the context of whole-person worship which engages the emotions.
2. Strong preaching is interpersonal communication which is seldom if ever merely intellectual, but is instead charged with the emotional impact of what is being said.
3. Strong preaching builds on a conflict's capacity to arouse emotion by presenting sharply contrasting alternatives where appropriate.
4. Strong preaching communicates the powerful whole-person impact of the Gospel appeal from which emotion cannot and should not be excluded.

"You were preaching to me today, Pastor!" people have sometimes said to me. The truth is I was NOT preaching to them specifically. I don't believe in aiming at any one person or groups of people. But God's Spirit was using what was being said to speak God's Word to them personally.

"I said 'Yes' to Jesus after last Sunday's sermon," a woman announced to me after one Sunday service. "Where did you do that?" I inquired. "Out in the parking lot," she replied. Without public display, she responded to the sermon of that morning by making a life transforming decision.

I recently heard Will Willimon reflect on his days as Dean of Chapel at Duke University. "I watched some preachers do everything right," related Willimon. "But the sermon fell to the ground without much impact. Then I watched as a preacher seemed to do a lot of things wrong. But the preached message connected powerfully because God's Spirit was clearly at work."

We often don't hear or know what has happened as a result of our preaching. But God has chosen to work through this method of incarnational communication to speak to men and women of all times and places. So we give God the best we have to offer in preparation to preach. We invest in having something worthwhile to say. And we work hard at saying it well. Then God accomplishes God's own purposes in the hearts and lives of hearers.

Reflection

1. This Sunday, or on religious TV, as you watch preaching unfold, observe delivery characteristics.
2. Which were assets to the communication? How and why?
3. Which were liabilities to the communication? How and why?
4. What were the emotional components of the preaching? How did you respond to them?
5. How can you learn from this observation of what to do or not to do?

Appendix A
Having Something to Say and Saying It Well at Weddings and Memorials

I HAVE FOUND serving at weddings and memorials or funeral services a fulfilling, but a very challenging part of ministry. These involve handling the deep and often on-the-edge emotions elicited by these intense experiences. Choreographing the event so people move in planned and appropriate ways is another aspect. Using liturgy that both links the event with the broader church community, and also speaks to those present also presents a challenge. And finding a music selection fit for a church/sacred ceremony is another task.

But the minister's primary job at most weddings and memorials/funerals is the meditation or homily. After I discovered that one definition of "homily" is "a tedious exhortation on some obscure moral point," I found myself opting for "meditation."

I have gently insisted to family members that I or another pastoral leader should say something which deals with why we are here and why we do what we do in these special services. Increasingly in my part of the country, these events are held outside a church context. Sometimes even when the event is held in a church building, the expressed desire is to shape it merely around the person who has died or around the couple getting married.

But when couples choose to be married in a church, what are they really saying? Should we not understand this event as a sacred ceremony which lifts up marriage? Should we not explain what covenant vows, taken before God and community, really mean? When we hold a memorial or funeral service in the church building, is that merely a convenience to family and friends, or should it speak something uniquely Christian?

Wedding Meditation

First, let me suggest some things to avoid.

Avoid a full-length sermon, exhausting bride, groom, and wedding party. This is not a forty-five minute exposition of some Bible passage, as one of my academic colleagues used to insist on doing. I asked a groom how long he thought the meditation should be. He responded, "Maybe ten minutes. But if you happen to say something worthwhile in five, you can quit then!" I usually aim at about ten minutes.

Avoid merely reflecting on your knowledge of bride and groom. Of course, a wedding meditation can and should be personal. But is its goal to be cute and sentimental? Or is its goal to say something from God about what is happening at this event? The purpose of a Christian wedding meditation is to set the context of what we believe about marriage and the marriage covenant.

If this is so, I recommend the following.

Let the meditation help the couple and wedding party to relax. Gentle and brief humor helps everyone to take a deep breath after what are often intense emotions. I often say, "I have good news for bride and groom and their families. You don't have to plan a wedding any more!"

Or I may reflect on what makes a marriage work. "Does marriage work merely because of compatibility? I don't think so. I believe that a man and a woman are fundamentally incompatible. Have you noticed that?"

The one bringing the meditation should specifically indicate its purpose. "It is my challenge and opportunity to point to the spiritual and Christian significance of what we are doing here today."

Let the meditation speak not only to bride and groom, but also to the gathered community. A Christian wedding is not merely a private ceremony orchestrated by bride and groom, but a public service of covenant making in the presence of God and the community.

Make sure the meditation reflects on a passage of Scripture. Often a bride and groom will have a particular passage read in the wedding service. If possible, I use that passage to speak to the significance of what we are doing.

Vital passages include:

- Genesis 2:18-25
- Ecclesiastes 4:9-12
- Song of Solomon 8:6-7
- 1 Corinthians 13 (Be sure to indicate that this was not written to couples but to church people and includes important principles for any human relationship.)
- Ephesians 5:21-33 (Note the passage begins at verse 21 and the injunction to submit to one another. In fact, the passage goes back to verse 18 and the challenge to be filled with the Spirit.)
- Colossians 3:12-15

Let the meditation lead into and prepare for the high and holy moment of covenant making. Here is where I usually affirm to the couple that their lives will never be the same after these next moments. At the same time, if they keep the doors of their lives open to God's Spirit, God will help them keep the powerful covenant into which they are about to enter.

Funeral or Memorial Service

I found myself much more at ease in this setting when I resolved what I believed to be the primary purpose of such a service. Since then, I often state some version of this purpose up front in the opening, welcoming words of the service.

The purpose of a Christian memorial or funeral is to tell the story of what God has done for us and the story of the person who has died.

Without telling the story of what God has done for us, a memorial service can be primarily sentimental. Without telling the story of the person who has died, the service can be sterile. Both stories are essential.

I suggest that the service itself be shaped around these two stories. Usually we begin with the story of God, through Scripture, prayer, song, and meditation. Then, and only then, do we move to a time of sharing memories of the one who has died.

This means that the funeral or memorial service meditation is not primarily a tribute to the one who has died. Though it will usually include personal references, its main purpose is to reflect on the meaning of this time for those who are living.

Again, I recommend that the ten to twelve minute meditation be Scripture based. In the case of a person of deep faith, the message can highlight our common hope in "the resurrection of the body and the life everlasting." In the case of one about whose faith we are unsure, we can highlight the offer of God's love in the midst of our pain and loss.

There are many other things which are said outside the pastoral meditation at these special-event services. But the meditation gives the opportunity and challenge to speak for God and for the Christian community into one of these key life-changing moments. Here also it is important that we have something to say and say it well.

Appendix B
Two Sample Sermons

BOTH SERMONS OFFERED below, based in different Bible passages, are focused on the theme of hope. The first sermon proceeds mostly deductively and is shaped in a linear manner. The second is more inductive and shaped organically. But inductive and deductive elements can be found in both cases. Both are rooted in Scripture passages, but have attempts to hook audience attention early. I included brief notes in italics calling attention to what is happening homiletically in the sermons and an upfront statement of the big idea.

I use these sermons I have prepared and delivered, not because they are models or masterpieces. However, I know my own sermons best—and don't have to obtain permission to publish them!

As you read, assess how what has been described earlier in this book is implemented in these real-life sermons. Also remember, you don't have to preach the same way. But I encourage you to ask yourself, What can I learn to further develop my own preaching style?

"Hope in Hard Times"
Romans 15:7-13

Big idea: biblical hope is rooted in what God has done, what God promised, and what we trust God to do now through the presence of the Holy Spirit.

The hook for this sermon includes sports news (now old) and lines from a Broadway musical. Notice formatting of shorter sentences which run down the page.

Big headlines this Wednesday, "Mariner's hopes fade as Griffey nears deal with Braves."
But the very next day the front page headlined the Mariners' deal with Griffey.
"The Mojo is back!" someone declared.
Now, it will be great for Ken Griffey Jr. to play again in Seattle.
But is that what will fulfill Mariners' hopes to win again?
(As we now know, Griffey was not the solution to the Mariners' woes!)
Don't we tend to think of hope as the vision of a winning season?
And the guy with the engaging grin and useful long ball is the guy who will make that hope come true. Right? Maybe!
Annie is a rags-to-riches, feel-good story of an orphan adopted by rich-guy Daddy Warbucks. Here's one of Annie's heart-warming songs:

"The sun will come out tomorrow
So you got to hang on till tomorrow
Come what may. Tomorrow! Tomorrow!
I love ya tomorrow.
You're only a day away."
Isn't that nice?! Doesn't that just warm your heart?
Annie is a story full of good feelings and positive expectations.
Some might say it's a story full of hope.
"Things are going to turn out all right. You'll see!"

Two Sample Sermons

Hope is a really big word these days. Our president wrote a book about hope.
We are encouraged to hope that financial hard times will not be here for too long.
We hope that the stock market will rebound, and jobs will return. We hope that our soldiers will come home from Iraq and Afghanistan.
We hope that things will get better.

Notice the following questions designed to connect with where people are and then to move toward a deeper and more biblical vision of hope. Questions help us open up a subject and begin to get at its core.

Don't we think of hope in terms of a winning season, bluer skies, better days?
Don't we equate hopefulness with optimism?
But is that what the Bible means by hope? Is it?
I try to be an optimist, a person whose glass is half full rather than half empty.
But often realism demands I recognize the glass really *is* only half full, not overflowing.
An optimist, I read somewhere, "is a guy that has never had much experience."
According to Mark Twain, "A man who is a pessimist before forty-eight knows too much; if he is an optimist after it, he knows too little."
There is a merely secular optimism.
And sometimes that kind of optimism is not very realistic.
But there's also a biblical hopefulness, which is what I want to ponder today.

We move now from life and questions about hope to the Scripture passage and its context. This next section orients listeners to the passage on which the sermon is based.

Romans 15 points to hope as a key ingredient in Christian community.

In Romans 14 and 15, Paul prays for the faith community in Rome that they will live in harmony with one another.
This harmony is based not just in good feelings about each other, but in who God is, the God of steadfastness and encouragement.
This harmony is one passion lived out in shared worship and results in glory to God.
In addition to harmony, Paul prays that believers in Rome will experience hope.
Christian community *is* to be a hope-filled, hope-based community.
But the hope Paul prays for is not just a winning season, Griffey or no-Griffey!
The hope Paul prays for is not just bluer skies and a better economy.
The hope for which Paul prays is not just optimism.

The introduction continues by briefly describing what this passage meant to those who first heard it. Remember that the Bible was first written to first-century people, not to us.

Remember, Paul is writing to Christ-followers who live in Caesar's neighborhood.
Caesar has declared that *he* is Lord, the *only* lord.
Anyone like Paul, who dares declare that someone besides Caesar is Lord, might just as well be thumbing his nose at the Roman Emperor.
And Caesar does not take well to having people thumb their noses at him.
When Paul writes to Roman believers about Jesus as the one who *"rises to rule the nations,"* he is making a theological statement.
But it's a theological statement with profound political implications.
Some people say preachers should confine themselves to theological statements.
But theological statements are likely to have huge political implications.
A statement that Jesus is Lord had immense political implications in first-century Rome.

Two Sample Sermons

Jesus as Lord sets up confrontation that's not going to make things easy for believers.
From history, we know that things in Rome did *not* get better for Christians.
In fact, they got worse for quite a long time.
So when Paul prays for hope, he's not just praying for a cheery outlook on life.
Hope in Romans is not just wishful thinking that things are going to get better.
Biblical hope, in fact, is not rooted in the circumstances of life.
Biblical hope is based in a deeper reality, the reality of who God is.

Here is the first glimpse of and reference to the big idea. It is reiterated again at the end of the section.

What Paul prays for the Christian community in Rome is a vision fixed on what God *has* done, what God *will* do, and on resources for *today* God has given them.
These are the basis for the hopefulness Paul prays will fill the community of believers.
This is the kind of hope which, says Paul, includes joy and peace in believing.
So a Christian community living out its faith in hard times is filled with hope.
But it's not just hopefulness defined by Hollywood or a feel-good musical like *Annie*.
It's not just the hopefulness of a Mumbai "slumdog" trying to win a million Rupees.
It's not just hope defined by our new president as "reclaiming the American dream."
"Reclaiming the American dream" is a worthy goal.
But it's not the same as biblical hope.
Biblical hope is rooted in what God has done, what God has promised, and what we trust God to do now through the presence of the Holy Spirit.

The message moves here from lengthy introduction which raised the question about what hope is and began to describe it in terms of the passage. The message now moves through a three-point structure with each emphasis stated in parallel fashion with one key, alliterative word. Alliteration isn't essential and shouldn't be forced, but it is memorable.

I. So the first thing I hear Paul urging as he prays for hope is *remember*.
    Remember the story.
    Remember the story of what God has done in Jesus.
    Jesus was Messiah of the Jews.
    But Jesus has now become Messiah for Gentiles as well.

Here again, we are reflecting on the context of the passage. Always take a Scripture passage in its context.

> This is the heart of Paul's complex argument plus a series of Old Testament quotes in 8-11 of Romans 15.
> Jesus did not come for the people of Israel alone.
> Jesus came also for Gentiles, for non-Jews.
> Thus, Gentiles and Jews should not look down on or judge one another in the Christian community despite their differences.
> Paul pleads for acceptance of one another despite differences.

Gentiles and Jews should join together in "one voice" worship of God because of what God has done for us all in Jesus.

> "Rejoice O Gentiles, with His people ... Praise the Lord, all you Gentiles, and let all the peoples praise Him" (9-10).

> People of every race and nation have become part of the Messiah's community.
> So remember the great story of God's ancient people of Israel.
> Remember the story of what God has done in Jesus not only for Israel, but for *all* people. Remember the story.

Two Sample Sermons

We are not required to stick to the text only. Here, the morning's Psalms reading is drawn in as illustration of the first main emphasis.

> In our psalm for this morning, Psalm 77, the poet sounds like a twenty-first century American who's lost a job or had his or her house value or retirement plan go south.
> The psalm writer is obviously going through hard times.
> The psalmist complains and laments to God about the hard things in his life.
> "I think of God, and I moan; I meditate and my spirit faints" (77:3).
> He describes his insomnia. He peppers God with questions.
>
> "Will the Lord ... never again be favorable?
> Has his steadfast love ceased for ever? Are his promises at an end for all time?
> Has God forgotten to be gracious? Has he in anger shut up his compassion..." (77:7-9)
>
> What a way to talk to God!
> We might say, "Hey man, get a grip!"
> But the psalmist takes us with him on his journey through hard times.
> The psalmist pours out his troubled feelings to God.
> But he continues,
>
> "I will call to mind the deeds of the Lord; *I will remember* your wonders of old. I will meditate on all your work, and muse on your mighty deeds..." (77:10)
>
> As the troubled poet remembers, he is able to turn from lament to praise.
>
> "Your way, O God, is holy! What god is so great as our God? You are the God who works wonders;
> You have displayed your might among the peoples..." (77:13-14)

Remembering what God has done leads to hopefulness.
And hopefulness is trust that the God of the ancient story is still the God of today.
One of the things we do in corporate worship is to remember our story.
We affirm the story of God's People.
Most of all, we affirm the story of what God has done for us in Jesus.
That's one reason I think people ought to be in worship regularly and often.
We need to join with the community in affirming the story which tells us who we are.
The story begins in Advent, Christmas, Epiphany, continues in Lent toward Holy Week.
Next Sunday, we begin the annual retelling of that part of the story leading to the cross and resurrection of Jesus.
The worship of the community is the Body retelling the great story.
When times are hard, God's community remembers the story of what God has done.
So don't forget the story of God's faithfulness.
Don't forget the story of God's coming to His People and to all People in Jesus.
Don't forget the story of Jesus' death, resurrection, ascension, and His promised return.
We are people of the story. And in hard times and under pressure, we turn to our story.
We are not just people of rules and regulations.
We are not just people of the dos and don'ts.
We are people of Good News, the Good News of what God has done for us in Jesus.
That is why we are people of hope.

Notice the transition phrases, which are like verbal signposts to assist people in following the structure.

But there is another dimension of hope suggested in Paul's great prayer.

Two Sample Sermons

    We are urged to look to the past as we remember the story.

II. But we are also urged to *Refocus*
Refocus on God's great future contained in God's promises.
In Christian community we have a past, a great story.
But we also have a great future which grows from our story.
Paraphrasing Isaiah 11:10, Paul declares "in Him the Gentiles shall hope" (Romans 15:12).
The prophet Isaiah has been talking about how "a shoot" shall spring from what seems like an unpromising "stump of Jesse."
And that shoot will grow to be a branch that in Isaiah's vision, will impact the world.
Isaiah launches a poetic vision of God's promised future of peace and wholeness.

> The wolf shall live with the lamb; the leopard shall lie down with the kid,
> The calf and the lion and the fatling together, and a little child shall lead them.
> They will not hurt or destroy on all my holy mountain; for the earth will be full of the knowledge of the Lord as the waters cover the sea.
> —Is. 11:6-8

Wow! That is not the way things are right now. True?
But this *is* what God intends for this earth and its inhabitants.
Even as we struggle with the way things are, we do not lose sight of what God has promised will be in God's great future.

Jeremiah is used as a biblical illustration of the second main emphasis."Once upon a time" sets the stage for storytelling. Notice the use of present-tense verbs in story telling.

    Once upon a time, long ago, there was this preacher named Jeremiah.
    Jeremiah is not an optimistic, feel-good preacher.

Jeremiah would never make it big on twenty-first century TV.
Jeremiah spends a lot of time bemoaning what he sees ahead for his people.
Things are absolutely awful for the people of Israel and are going to get worse.
But despite being a weeping prophet, Jeremiah is a hopeful preacher. Really!
One of the symbolic acts God tells Jeremiah to do is to go buy a field in time of war.
Here's the army of Babylon besieging Jerusalem.
Here's Jeremiah himself under guard in the king's palace.
But God instructs Jeremiah to exercise his option to buy a field.
That field is probably right then being trampled under foot by enemy soldiers.
Jeremiah cries out to God,

> See the siege ramps have been cast up against the city to take it, and the city, faced with sword, famine, and pestilence, has been given into the hands of the Chaldeans who are fighting against it …
> Yet you, O Lord God, have said to me, "Buy the field for money and get witnesses"—though the city has been given into the hands of the Chaldeans."
>
> —32:24-25

Jeremiah's hope-filled conclusion,

> Houses and fields and vineyards shall again be bought in this land.

Jeremiah's purchase of a field was not just a savvy economic transaction, like buying stock when the price is low.
Jeremiah was symbolically engaging in hopefulness because he believed in God's future.
Jeremiah saw beyond hard times to God's purposes to bring His people back to this land.
Jeremiah was not an optimist as we think of optimists.
Jeremiah recognized that things were going to get worse.

Two Sample Sermons

But Jeremiah was hopeful because he believed in God's good purpose for His people.

To be what God wants us to be in the midst of crisis, we need a living trust in what God has in mind for the future.

But God's future is not just the end of an economic crisis, return of a bull stock market, rebounding property values, or easing of credit.

What God has promised is that *God's* purposes will be fulfilled in God's world.

We need to be really clear on this!

When we hear prosperity preachers promise good times, more wealth, better jobs, etc., maybe we wish that were true. We would like for it to be that way!

But hope for God's people is based on God's priorities, not just our prosperity.

What we want most is for God's will and God's purpose to be fulfilled in the earth.

Jesus said, "Seek first the kingdom of God and His righteousness and all these things (the stuff that we need for every day life) will be given to you as well" (Matthew 6:33).

God's people can be hopeful amid economic distress because financial prosperity is not the ultimate vision we're focused on.

God has greater plans for the world than the prosperity of our IRAs or 401c3s.

God has bigger purposes for the world than our own economic prosperity.

So one way to be hopeful in today's crisis is to refocus our vision on what God wants and what God has planned for His future.

And because we believe what God has promised, our vision of the present is transformed.

We are rooted in our story.

We are refocused on God's great future.

Thus, we can be hopeful amid hard times.

There's one more aspect to Paul's vision of hope for faith community in Rome.

We've looked backward and remembered our story.

We've looked forward and refocused our vision on what God has planned and promised.
But biblical hope is not just bound by the past or fixated on a pie-in-the-sky future.

III. There's a third word for the vision not of yesterday or tomorrow but today. And that word is *rely*.
Rely on the Holy Spirit in the here and now of our lives.

The sermon ties each of the main emphases to the big idea and to the Scripture passage.

Paul prays that believers in Rome will "abound in hope by the power of the Holy Spirit."
The Holy Spirit is the Spirit of God and the Spirit of Jesus living in believers.
It is the Spirit who even in hard times fills us "with all joy and peace in believing."
It is the Spirit who helps us remember what God has done for us in Jesus.
It is the Spirit who helps us fix our vision on God's great future, which is bigger and better even than an economic recovery plan.
It is the Spirit who enables us in the midst of hard times to experience joy and peace and abounding hope.
As a Christian community, we are challenged to remember our story, refocus on God's great future, and rely on the Spirit in our present-day lives.

Illustrations are important. This illustration moves toward the conclusion.

A young soldier lost both his legs in battle.
Something died within this young man when he thought he would never walk again.
He stared at the ceiling, wouldn't talk, refused to cooperate with doctors or nurses.

Two Sample Sermons

One day another hospital inmate came by and sat down near this soldier's bed.

He began playing softly on a harmonica. That was all for that day.

Next day the player came again and again. They talked a little more each day. One day the harmonica player played a lively tune and began to do a tap dance.

The soldier looked on but was apparently unimpressed.

"Hey, why don't you smile once and let the world know you're alive!" the dancer said with a friendly smile.

But the legless soldier responded, "I might as well be dead because of the fix I'm in."

"Okay," answered his happy friend, "so you're dead. But you're not as dead as a fellow who was crucified two thousand years ago, and He came out of it all right."

"Oh, it's easy for you to preach," replied the patient, "but if you were in my fix, you'd sing a different tune."

The dancer responded, "I know a two-thousand-year-old resurrection is pretty far in the dim past. So maybe an up-to-date example will help you believe it can be done."

He pulled up his pant legs so the young man in the bed could see two artificial limbs.

The tap-dancing fellow with the harmonica was not simply a Pollyanna.

He once lay where that young soldier now lay. He had known the power of a resurrection.

He had learned to live life abundantly, hopefully—even without legs.

Conclusion continues with applications to current life situations.

Some of us struggle with hopefulness about the economy, our finances, our work situation, maybe even our marriage.

Christian hope is not just wishing and waiting for things to get better.

Christian hope is not held hostage by the circumstances of our lives.

Christian hope is not just some preacher shouting, "Be hopeful! Look on the bright side."

Christian hope is trusting God and living in relationship with God's Son right in the midst of hard times.

Christian hope is believing in the great story of Jesus' death, resurrection, and promised return.

Christian hope is living today in the light of that promised future.

Christian hope is allowing the Spirit to give us new legs, even dancing legs in the midst of whatever has happened to us.

And Christian hope is a choice.

Hope is a choice to remember what God has done and refocus on what God promises.

Hope is a choice to be open to the Spirit of Hope in our here and now.

Hope is not something that happens to us. We choose hope and keep choosing.

Two Sample Sermons

"Undated Hope"

Isaiah 11:1-9; Romans 15:4-6

Big Idea: Undated hope, i.e., hope without timelines shapes our lives in the here and now even while we wait for the complete fulfillment of our hope.

Family vignettes get attention. This one may pique people's curiosity even though it doesn't move immediately into the theme.

I was talking to our son who then lived in Fairbanks, Alaska.
"Anna has a question about the Bible," he said to me.
Anna is their eight-year-old daughter in third grade in a Christian school.
Leading up to Christmas, third graders were assigned to read a chapter of Isaiah per night.
Anna and her mother were struggling with rather vivid sexual imagery in some of Isaiah.
"What's that all about?" they wanted to know from the supposed Bible expert.
Isaiah, as a whole I think, is not ideal third-grade reading material.
Last week my brother was visiting from Phoenix.
He too is reading Isaiah during Advent. He too is not having an easy time of it.
Lots of judgment and doom was his assessment.
Have you tried to read all of Isaiah recently? There's a lot of heavy-duty stuff in Isaiah.
Much of it feels foreign to our twenty-first century lives.
That is not surprising since it was written between 2,500 and 2,700 years ago, in a dramatically different time and place from twenty-first century USA.
Why then read Isaiah during the season of Advent?
Why does the lectionary, which we are following these Sundays, assign Isaiah passages to be read in Advent?
Why assign the whole book of Isaiah to be read by eight and nine year olds?

Something to Say ? Say It Well !

There are in Isaiah passages of wonderful beauty and power.
And many of these passages are about Messiah.
Last Sunday afternoon, I sat in the balcony while the wonderful music of Handel's *Messiah* washed over me.
Many of those words come straight out of the King James Version of Isaiah.
This vision of Messiah pierces the doom and gloom of some of Isaiah.
This vision of Messiah breaks through the ancient figures of speech.
This vision of Messiah is a vision of hope in very hard and dark times.

"Just imagine" invites listeners to identify with the situation of Bible people. This is followed up by context material.

Just imagine a time of deep darkness for us as Americans.
Imagine, just imagine, Washington DC destroyed.
Imagine the capitol building razed to the ground.
Imagine monuments to Washington and Jefferson and Lincoln broken down.
Imagine the impact on our American psyche.
Then imagine having to be deported a few hundred miles away from our homeland to live in the land of our enemies. Imagine!
A recent *60 Minutes* program depicted the plight of Christians in post Saddam Hussein Iraq.
Saddam Hussein was an evil man. But he did tolerate Christianity.
Pre-war Iraq had the largest percentage of Christians among Middle Eastern countries.
But militant Islamic groups have targeted Christians and churches.
Most Christians in Iraq have witnessed the destruction of their churches and have had to flee their homeland to other countries.
Many, many Iraqi Christians are now dead or in exile.
It's a dark and difficult time for Iraqi believers.
Now think of what people who first heard and read Isaiah were going through.
The first half of Isaiah envisions the rising power of Assyria about 700 years before Christ.

Two Sample Sermons

Assyrians were nasty, harsh, cruel people from the Mesopotamian Valley.
Eventually Assyria swooped down, defeated, and deported the ten northern tribes of Israel.
During this time period, Isaiah preaches and teaches in the two southern tribes of Judah centered in Jerusalem.
They were not swallowed up by Assyria as were their neighbors to the north.
But Judah lived in fear of the same thing happening to them.
So it was a dark, dark time.
The last half of Isaiah, beginning at chapter 40, envisions a later time when the southern kingdom of Judah, including the city of Jerusalem and its temple were destroyed.
Just imagine the impact of that scenario!
God's people were taken into exile not to Assyria, but to Babylon, present-day Iraq.
Along with the exodus from Egypt, the Babylonian exile was a defining period for the ancient Hebrew people.
But after a few decades, and after regime change in Babylon, a tolerant Persian Emperor allowed Jews to return from exile and rebuild their city and temple.
This is the story of Ezra and Nehemiah.
So there was still hope for God's people.
Isaiah 40 speaks words of encouragement and hope. "Comfort, O comfort my people, says your God. Speak tenderly to Jerusalem" (40:1).

The introduction moves toward the big idea theme, suggested in the title. We define a little of what "undated hope" is, but do not offer a linear, propositional outline. After the opening, the structure looks something like a wagon wheel, with spokes moving between the rim and the hub which is the theme.

Periodically in Isaiah, there are breakthroughs of hope, hope in the midst of darkness.
But hope in Isaiah is what one scholar has called *undated hope!*

This is a phrase that has gripped me this week. *Undated hope!* This is light in the midst of darkness.
This is promise of God's faithfulness.
But there's no guarantee of when what you hope for will come to pass.
Undated hope!
Says the writer of Proverbs, "Hope deferred makes the heart sick" (13:12).
It's hard to wait for what we hope for, especially if we have no timeline for the fulfillment of our hope.
Aren't we people who want dates and timelines and schedules?
God, you see this thing in my life that bothers me, this trouble I have.
You need to take care of it. And you need to take care of it *now*.
God, you see this addiction, this disease, this depression I deal with.
You need to get rid of it for me, and you need to do it *now*.
God, you see this thing I've been praying about for so long.
Why have you not answered my prayer?
"Undated hope," writes a biblical scholar, "is a living, ever-present assurance for God's people."
"And," he continues, "it is at this point that … (Isaiah) speaks as much to the church today as in Isaiah's time" (Motyer, p. 120).
Undated hope!
Last Sunday we heard the vision of Isaiah 2.

> They shall beat their swords into ploughshares, and their spears into pruning hooks;
> Nation shall not lift up sword against nation, neither shall they learn war any more.

What a vision that is! But it's an undated vision.
Even today we don't see it happening. There's no timeline, no schedule.
This morning, from today's passage in chapter 11:6,

> The wolf shall live with the lamb, the leopard shall lie down with the kid, the calf and the lion and the fatling together, and

Two Sample Sermons

> a little child shall lead them ... They will not hurt or destroy on all my holy mountain.
> The earth will be full of the knowledge of the Lord as the waters cover the sea.

Wow! What a vision! But it's undated.
In the Isaiah 11 passage, there is a progression, a journey.
The journey begins back in the familiar vision of Isaiah 6:8.
This is the prophet's vision of a holy God who calls Isaiah into ministry.

> I heard the voice of the Lord saying, 'Whom shall I send, and who will go for us?'
> And I said, "Here am I, send me!" And God said, "Go and say to this people:"

But what was the message Isaiah was to speak?
Isaiah was not to preach a prosperity gospel or a feel-good message.
Isaiah, like Jeremiah and other Old Testament prophets, wouldn't make it on TV!
Isaiah was to preach a vision of doom and gloom.

> Until cities lie waste without inhabitant, and houses without people, and the land is utterly desolate; until the Lord sends everyone far away, and vast is the emptiness in the midst of the land.

Wow! If that was the message I had to preach, I might not have signed up to be a pastor!
Isaiah 6 concludes by picturing a tree stump which remains standing in the midst of ruins.
What does a stump say to us?
A stump is a vision of something cut down.
A stump envisions the end of something.
A stump does not seem like a hope-filled picture.
Stumps are what litter many of our lives.
Stumps are good things that seem to have come to an end.

Stumps are dreams and expectations that have not materialized.
Stumpville is not a very hopeful place to live.
Do any of us know anything about living in Stumpville?
But says the last verse of Isaiah 6, "The holy seed is its stump."
Seed *is* a picture of hope. A seed promises a plant, a new tree, new fruit.
In the stump is the seed of something hopeful and fruitful.
Journey on to Isaiah 11. "A shoot will come up."
From where?
"From the stump of Jesse and a branch shall grow out of his roots."
There *is* hope, hope even in Stumpville.
But it is *undated hope.*
There is promise, but no schedule.
There is anticipation, but no timeline.
Hope in Stumpville, according to Isaiah, comes in a person whom God will send.
God's hope-filled work is almost always brought about through a person or people.
God had worked through descendants of David to lead and guide His people.
Kings who followed David had been a mixed lot, some good, several bad.
But God would work through a future descendant of David's line.
God would work through the Anointed One, Messiah.

> The spirit of the Lord shall rest upon Him, the spirit of wisdom and understanding, the spirit of counsel and might, the spirit of knowledge and the fear of the Lord.

It is this Anointed One whose coming to earth we anticipate in the Advent Season.
And it is through the work of this Anointed One, this Messiah that the hopeful vision of earth filled with the knowledge of the Lord will come to be.
But again, this is an *undated hope.*
There's no guarantee of when, no timeline, no schedule.

Two Sample Sermons

We have continued to circle in to the theme from the Isaiah material. Now, we paint a more contemporary picture illustrating the theme.

I've been to Yellowstone National Park once. Years later what I remember most are the geysers.
Oh yes, we watched Old Faithful erupt every hour or so. Very predictable!
But there was another geyser, bigger, more dramatic, but not at all regular.
If you can believe it, I sat and watched and waited for a couple hours while this geyser gurgled and bubbled up and then settled back down and then started all over again.
Finally, this geyser (whose name I cannot remember) erupted with dramatic impact.
The awesome sight was worth the wait.
I remember the sign posted by the National Park Service.
It said, "We predict but we do not schedule."
We would like not only to predict, but to schedule God's activity in our lives and world.
We would like God to operate on our timetable.
But God is God! We do not, and cannot, schedule God.
And most of God's promises to us involve this *undated hope*.

Into the mix we throw some general reflections on the meaning of hope from a biblical perspective.

Hope in the Bible is not the same thing we usually think of as hope.
"Did you pass your finals?"
"I hope so."
"Will Santa bring you what you want for Christmas?"
"I hope so!"
That may very well be wishful thinking.
Biblical hope is not wishful thinking but confident expectation.

Here is the big idea and its development.

Biblical hope is based first in what God *has done*.
Hope begins by looking backward.
God had brought blessing from the family of Jesse, the father of David, says Isaiah 11:1.
The family of David was the root.
The family of David represents what God had done.
Biblical hope, confident expectation, is based in a backward look to what God has done.
But biblical hope also looks forward to what *God will do*.
What God has done gives promise of what God will do.
Follow Isaiah on to the great vision of chapter 65: "I am about to create new heavens and a new earth ... Be glad and rejoice forever in what I am creating" (65:17).
Our minds leap ahead to the vision of Revelation, a vision of what God is going to do.
But biblical hope also shapes what we do and how we live *in the here and now*.
Biblical hope is not just about history.
Biblical hope is not just for the sweet by and by.
Biblical hope shapes our lives in the here and now.
Despite living with *undated hope*, we believe in God's faithful presence.
And God's presence makes all the difference in how we cope with life today.
Our hope, even though undated, shapes our lives in the here and now.

Sometimes, it's useful to give people specific directions about following the roadmap of the less linear sermon. What follows are New Testament illustrations of "undated hope."

Are you still with me? Please hang with me as I take you briefly from Isaiah to Romans.
Centuries after Isaiah, the apostle Paul writes to house churches in Rome.

Two Sample Sermons

Paul tells the mix of Hebrews and Gentiles in the Roman church that the things in the Hebrew Bible were written down "for our instruction."
And what is the outcome of this instruction? "So that by steadfastness and by the encouragement of the Scriptures *we might have hope*!" (Romans 15:4).
Paul goes on to paint a very hope-filled picture of the believing community.

> May the God of steadfastness and encouragement grant you to live in harmony with one another, in accordance with Christ Jesus, so that together you may with one voice glorify the God and Father of our Lord Jesus Christ.
> —Romans 15:5-6

What a wonderful vision of Christian community, of believers living in harmony, of glory and honor coming to God.
What a vision! What a hope!
But do you suppose that is the way church life was in these Roman house churches?
We know that most of the churches to which Paul wrote had problems.
That's an important reason why Paul wrote these letters.
The church in Corinth, for example, had *big* problems and lots of problems.
In the Corinthian church, believers did not get along with fellow believers.
At church potlucks, folks who could afford beef roasts sat in one area and would not share with people who couldn't even afford hamburger.
People who had mystical experiences with the Lord felt themselves superior to people whose relationship with God was mundane and everyday.
People who came from Jewish backgrounds had a hard time with non-Jews, with Gentiles.
There was hope of harmony, but not always the reality of harmony among God's people.

What Paul was expressing in Romans 15 is *undated hope*.
When we hire new staff at church, I usually give them a little talk.
It's called the,"This is a great place to work, but it's not heaven" talk.
I tell new staff members that church people, including fellow staff members will often be wonderful and godly and great to work with.
But once in a while church people can be demanding, troublesome, and difficult.
That goes for me too!
Sometimes, there is the temptation to become disillusioned with brothers and sisters in Christ.
I'm sure that's the way it was in Rome 2,000 years ago.
But Paul had high hopes for these "saints" as he calls them.
Paul even calls believers in the Corinthian church "saints"!
The goal of what God wants to do now in believers' everyday lives is the vision and the challenge of today.
But this is vision without timeline. This is promise without total fulfillment now.
But persevering in undated hope shapes us into what God wants.
The hope of harmony among believers helps us live that way.
The hope of a world at peace motivates us to be what Jesus called "peacemakers."
Undated hope shapes our lives in the here and now even while we wait for the complete fulfillment of our hope.

A seasonal reflection is added to the mix followed by a story leading to conclusion. The non-linear, more organic, structure takes people with the preacher on a journey without setting up a series of deductive and linear propositions or statements..

"Joy to the World" is one of the great carols of this season.
"Joy to the world, the Lord is come … Joy to the world the Savior reigns … He rules the world with truth and grace."
But there is little evidence from today's newspaper that Jesus indeed does rule the world.
The carol's vision involves statements of hope, but undated hope.

Two Sample Sermons

We believe in the reality of Christ's kingdom in the here and now.
We believe that this kingdom will one day come in completeness.
But we live without the complete fulfillment of that promise.
The third stanza of this great carol, however, makes our hope the shaper of our behavior.
"No more let sins and sorrows grow. No more let thorns infest the ground."
This is hope shaping behavior.
I hear the hymn writer urging us to let our great hope shape how we live today.
"No more let sins and sorrows grow. No more let thorns infest the ground.
He comes to make His blessings flow. Far as the curse is found."
Undated hope sets before us a vision that draws and pulls and motivates us even as we continue to wait for the complete fulfillment of what we hope for.
Virginia was nineteen and pregnant when she went to live with her fifteenth set of foster parents.
She sat silently in a chair, hands neatly clasped, staring into her lap. Finally, the foster mother said, "Are you frightened, Virginia?" "Kinda," she replied without looking up. Then, "I've been in lots of homes." "Well," the sympathetic woman tried to reassure this bewildered young mother-to-be, "Let's hope this time turns out for the best." Virginia's reply was flat delivered without even looking up.
"Hurts too much to hope," she said. "Hurts too much to hope."

The conclusion invites a range of hypothetical listeners to respond.

Maybe some of us understand that kind of pain. Do we?
Maybe some of us find it difficult to live in hope this Advent season.
Maybe some of us find it complicated to celebrate this season of hope.
I remind us that we know a God who has never given up on us. We know a God who sent His One and Only Son to become one of us.

"I am with you," says Jesus, "even while you wait for that undated hope to be fulfilled.
And I will never, ever leave you," said Jesus.
When we know a God like that, we can continue to hope no matter what.
When we know a God like that, we can live in hope even if there is no timeline.
When we know a God like that, we can live with undated hope.
Advent is the season of hope, undated, but yet real hope.
I close with Paul's great blessing at the end of the Romans 15 passage:

> May the God of hope fill you with all joy and peace in believing, so that you may abound in hope by the power of the Holy Spirit.
> —15:13

Amen!

Works Cited

Anderson, Kenton, 2006, *Choosing to Preach*, Grand Rapids: Zondervan.
Craddock, Fred, 2001, *As One Without Authority*, St Louis: Chalice Press.
Chilcote, Paul, 2004, *Recapturing the Wesleys' Vision*, Downers Grove: Intervarsity Press.
Demaray, Donald, 1990, *Introduction to Homiletics*, Grand Rapids: Baker Books.
Douthat, Ross, "Heaven and Nature" *New York Times*, December 20, 2009.
Garreau, Joel, 1981, *The Nine Nations of North America*, New York: Avon.
Hoch, Robert, "Saturday Night Special," *Preaching*, Nov/Dec, 2008.
Johnston, Graham, 2001, *Preaching to a Postmodern World*, Grand Rapids: Baker.
Leithart, Peter, "Of Preaching and Newspapers," *Biblical Horizons Newsletter*, 89 (1996).
Long, Thomas, 1989, *The Witness of Preaching*, Louisville: Westminster/John Knox Press.
Miller, Calvin, 1989, *Spirit, Word, Story*, Dallas: Word.

Miller, Calvin, 2006, *Preaching,* Grand Rapids: Baker Books.
Miller, Jeff, "Boring Your Church at the Speed of Sound," *Preaching,* March/April, 2003, p. 23-24
Pagitt, Doug, 2005, *Preaching Re-imagined,* Grand Rapids: Zondervan.
Peterson, Eugene, 1996, *Living the Message,* San Francisco: HarperCollins.
Pitt-Watson, Ian, 1986, *A Primer for Preachers,* Grand Rapids: Baker Books.
Quicke, Michael, 2006, *360 Degree Leadership,* Grand Rapids: Baker Books.
Robinson, Haddon, "Preaching the Gospel Today," *PreachingToday.com,* June 2, 2008.
Robinson, Haddon, "Better Big Ideas," *PreachingToday.com,* Audio Workshop, undated.
Robinson, Haddon, 1980, *Biblical Preaching,* Grand Rapids: Baker Books.
Sangster, William, 1958, *Power in Preaching,* London: Epworth Press.
Sittser, Gerald, 2010, *Water From a Deep Well,* Downers Grove: Intervarsity Press.
Spurgeon, Charles, undated, *Lectures to my Students,* London: Marshall Brothers, Ltd.
Sweazey, George, 1976, *Preaching the Good News,* Englewood Cliffs: Prentice-Hall.
Sweet, Leonard, 2007, *The Gospel According to Starbucks,* New York: Doubleday Religious Publishing Group.
Warren, Rick, "Tips for Concluding Your Sermons," *Rick Warren's Ministry Toolbox,* #342, December, 2007.
Willobee, Sondra, 2009, *The Write Stuff,* Louisville: Westminster/John Knox Press.
Wright, N.T. 2005, *The Last Word,* San Francisco: HarperCollins.

WinePressPublishing
Great Books, Defined.

To order additional copies of this book call:
1-877-421-READ (7323)
or please visit our website at
www.WinePressbooks.com

If you enjoyed this quality custom-published book,
drop by our website for more books and information.

www.winepresspublishing.com
"Your partner in custom publishing."

www.ingramcontent.com/pod-product-compliance
Lightning Source LLC
Chambersburg PA
CBHW071448160426
43195CB00013B/2050